A YORKSHIRE
MISCELLANY

A YORKSHIRE
MISCELLANY

TOM HOLMAN

FRANCES LINCOLN LIMITED
PUBLISHERS

For Mum and Dad

Frances Lincoln Limited
4 Torriano Mews
Torriano Avenue
London NW5 2RZ
www.franceslincoln.com

A Yorkshire Miscellany
Copyright © Frances Lincoln Limited 2008
Text copyright © Tom Holman 2008

First Frances Lincoln edition 2008

ISBN 978-0-7112-2865-8

Printed and bound in Singapore

2 4 6 8 9 7 5 3 1

A TWO-MINUTE HISTORY
OF YORKSHIRE

Yorkshire has had a fascinating, roller-coaster history, characterised in the thousand years or so between the departure of the Romans and the end of the Civil War by short, sharp upheavals followed by long periods of recovery and development.

Yorkshire's Stone Age hunters and gatherers would have found the area covered in forests and full of wildlife. From a few thousand years BC the forests began to be cut down for farming, before the Bronze Age brought tools and weapons. Celtic settlers arrived in Yorkshire around 500 BC, and the Romans in AD 71. The Roman forts were gradually succeeded by towns including York, the capital of the Roman north, the place that gave Yorkshire its name, and its centre of gravity to this day. Though they had a substantial impact on Yorkshire's infrastructure, the Romans were gone by the 5th century. Next came the Anglo-Saxons together with the arrival of Christianity and the start of trade, though life remained largely agricultural. And reasonably peaceful, too, until the Vikings landed, first raiding and then ruling Yorkshire for a century. They left Yorkshire with the word *threthingr,* meaning third part and later Riding, which was used to describe the three regions of Yorkshire: the North, West and East Ridings.

Harald Hardrada arrived from Norway in 1066, defeated by the English in some of the country's most famous battles. William of Normandy became king, but soon faced a rebellion from Yorkshire that he brutally suppressed in the 'Harrying of the North'. Recovering over the next few centuries, new towns, including Barnsley, Hull, Leeds and Sheffield, began to be established. The population rose, farming increased, and monasteries sprang up. But in the 14th century Yorkshire was hit by a triple whammy of famine, the Black Death and wars with the Scots. The next century brought the Wars of the Roses between the Houses of York and Lancaster, further decimating Yorkshire's towns and population.

Another spell of recovery followed, with agriculture and trades like wool and cloth enriching the region. Henry VIII's reformation and the dissolution of the monasteries brought more chaos, and in the 1640s Yorkshire was split by the Civil War. Over the next few centuries the identity and character of Yorkshire as we know it started to emerge. As industry flourished through the 18th century, towns sprawled and transport links improved, the railways in particular bringing previously remote areas much closer together. With heavier industries like coal and steel arriving, conditions in the towns and factories worsened, though by the late 19th century improvements to the water supply and public facilities were being made. More money and leisure accelerated the growth of seaside towns like Scarborough.

The decline of traditional industries into the early 20th century hit Yorkshire hard and forced it to find new ones. The Second World War brought more hardships and widespread bombing. Afterwards, immigration shook up Yorkshire's demographics, and in 1974 the reorganisation of local government borders sliced up Yorkshire's three Ridings into new counties for administrative purposes. These days Yorkshire is either broken down into its local authority regions or banded together with the Humber for statistical purposes.

Each of the rulers and visitors left their mark on Yorkshire, but its special identity has only strengthened over the centuries. Yorkshire has always been a state of mind as much as a physical entity, and loyalty to it is as strong as it has ever been.

THE YORKSHIRE CODE

The Yorkshire Ridings Society was set up in 1974 with the aim of preserving the identity of what its members consider to be the 'real' Yorkshire after the reorganisation of county boundaries. The society still considers the county to be made up of the North, East and West Ridings and campaigns for Yorkshire proper to be accurately represented on maps, road signs and addresses. The society also drew up 'The Yorkshire Code', seven tenets by which its members agree to stand.

Areas administered by local councils do not replace Yorkshire – they are purely administrative areas and can be altered or abolished at any time.

Never refer to the abolition of the Ridings of Yorkshire – this is not true.

Always use Yorkshire correctly – meaning the geographical county that has existed for over 1,100 years.

Wherever you live in Yorkshire, use a Yorkshire postal address, including the postcode.

Ensure that maps show the geographical boundaries of Yorkshire as well as the administrative ones. The Yorkshire borders are permanent.

If you are a Yorkshireman or woman, always insist on your
Yorkshire rights.

Ensure that children are taught the truth about Yorkshire and
are not denied access to their heritage and identity.

TEN AMUSING PLACE-NAMES

Some unusual places across Yorkshire, all featured on Ordnance Survey
maps, to the amusement of visitors if not the people who live there.

Blubberhouses (in the Washburn valley)

Booze (in Arkengarthdale)

Crackpot (in Swaledale)

Giggleswick (near Settle)

Idle (near Bradford)

Jump (near Barnsley)

Kettlesing Bottom (near Harrogate)

Land of Nod (near Holme-on-Spalding-Moor)

Wetwang (near Driffield)

Wham (near Settle)

THE STORY OF THE FLAT CAP

If there's one item of clothing that has identified Yorkshiremen most
closely over the years, it's the flat cap.

The classic cap is made of wool or tweed, with a little brim at the
front and a higher peak at the back. Some say its use can be traced back
as far as the 15th century, but it undoubtedly had its heyday in the
industrial England of the 19th and early 20th centuries, when the vast
majority of working-class men wore one virtually all the time. Flat caps
can be seen on every head in photos from the times of mills and factory
gates, as well as of sporting events. Featherstone Rovers, a rugby league
team in west Yorkshire, is still widely known as 'The Flat Cappers' after
the days when every fan donned one.

The flat cap has always been worn well beyond Yorkshire – and in many parts of Europe as well as Britain – but along with whippets and pigeons, it has become something of a stereotype of the working-class man in the northeast, thanks in part to its use by caricatured TV, film and cartoon people like Andy Capp. Falling use and rising costs of production led to the closure in 2000 of the Leeds factory of J.W. Myers, once the biggest cap maker and exporter in the world. Production then switched to the incongruous but considerably cheaper centre of Panyu in southern China.

Ironically, since this setback the flat cap has enjoyed something of a renaissance among young people, after being brought back into fashion by a number of celebrities. It still gets good use among rural men across Yorkshire, and among farmers in particular, who perhaps appreciate it more for keeping the head warm and dry than for its fashion appeal.

THE YORKSHIRE DALES IN NUMBERS

Some facts and figures about the Yorkshire Dales National Park.

259,612 . . . . .average house price in pounds in 2006
19,650 . . . . .population living within the boundaries
8,363 . . . . .household spaces
2,315 . . . . .highest point in feet (736 m) – Whernside
1954 .year the National Park was established
1,800 . . . . .listed buildings
1,302 . . . . .miles (2,095 km) of public footpaths and bridleways
685 . . . . .area in square miles (1,774 sq km) of the National Park
357 . . . . .square miles (925 sq km) of open country
304 . . . . .miles (490 km) of rivers
277 . . . . .square miles (717 sq km) of agricultural land
203 . . . . .scheduled ancient monuments
101 . . . . .sites of Special Scientific Interest
83 . . . . .parishes
62 .percentage of land defined as 'open access'
37 . . . . .conservation areas
29 . . . . .residents per square mile (2.6 sq km)
23 . . . . .square miles (60 sq km) of woodland
5 . . . . .National Nature Reserves
3 . . . . .square miles (7.7 sq km) of urban area
1 . . . . .square mile (2.6 sq km) of inland water

FAMOUS YORKSHIRE FOLK –
CAPTAIN JAMES COOK

Others may be better known, but few Yorkshiremen have done more for the wider world than Captain James Cook.

He was born in Marton in north Yorkshire (now part of the sprawl of Middlesbrough) in 1728. Sent to the fishing village of Staithes to be apprenticed in a shop, Cook soon became much more interested in the sea and moved to nearby Whitby to begin another apprenticeship in the merchant navy. For several years he helped to transport coal up and down the English coast, rising up through the ranks while learning the skills of seamanship. His rapid progression continued after he joined the Royal Navy in his late twenties, and after impressing the Admiralty and Royal Society with his surveying and mapping abilities, he was put in charge of his own ship, the *Endeavour*, for the first of his three great voyages in 1768.

Cook's three-year Pacific journey was intended to chart the transit of Venus across the Sun, but ended with him mapping all of the previously discovered New Zealand coastline and journeying on up the eastern coast of Australia, almost holing the ship on the Great Barrier Reef. After a year back home he set out again, this time with two ships, reaching the Antarctic Circle and charting various southern islands. The voyage proved wrong those in the Royal Society and elsewhere who believed there was a large continent south of Australia.

Cook found on his return that he had become renowned for his exploits, but he was soon back on the seas once more, this time attempting to cross from the Pacific to the Atlantic via the fabled Northwest Passage. On board the ship *Resolution*, Cook sailed to Hawaii and then up to chart the west coast of America. He died in 1779 on the return to Hawaii during a fight with islanders, aged 51.

Because Cook kept copious journals and was accompanied on his voyages by scientists and artists, much is known about his great adventures and discoveries. His skills in navigation and cartography, coupled with a great bravery and thirst for exploration, vastly advanced Britain's knowledge of the world, and he is also remembered across Australia and the Pacific through numerous memorials and buildings named in his honour. His Yorkshire links are preserved at the Captain Cook Museum in the building where he lodged as an apprentice on Whitby harbour. Though his birthplace is now long gone, Marton has the Captain Cook Birthplace Museum and there are various tributes and connections across Middlesbrough.

YORKSHIRE WRITERS

Forty of the county's most famous novelists, poets and playwrights, together with their places of birth.

John Arden (b.1930) – Barnsley

Simon Armitage (b.1963) – Huddersfield

Kate Atkinson (b.1951) – York

W.H. Auden (1907–73) – York

Pat Barker (b.1943) – Thornaby-on-Tees

Stanley Barstow (b.1928) – Horbury

Alan Bennett (b.1934) – Leeds

Gordon Bottomley (1874–1948) – Keighley

Malcolm Bradbury (1932–2000) – Sheffield

Barbara Taylor Bradford (b.1933) – Leeds

John Braine (1922–86) – Bradford

Anne (1820–49), Charlotte (1816–55) and Emily (1818–48) Brontë – all Thornton

A.S. Byatt (b.1936) – Sheffield

Bruce Chatwin (1940–89) – Sheffield

Roy Clarke (b.1930) – Austerfield

William Congreve (1670–1729) – Bardsey

Margaret Drabble (b.1939) – Sheffield

William Empson (1906–84) – Howden

Helen Fielding (b.1958) – Morley

George Gissing (1857–1903) – Wakefield

John Godber (b.1956) – Upton

Willis Hall (1929–2005) – Leeds

Joanne Harris (b.1964) – Barnsley

Tony Harrison (b.1937) – Leeds

Susan Hill (b.1942) – Scarborough

Barry Hines (b.1939) – Barnsley

Winifred Holtby (1898–1935) – Rudston

Ted Hughes (1930–98) – Mytholmroyd

Eric Knight (1897–1943) – Menston

Ian McMillan (b.1956) – Barnsley

Andrew Marvell (1621–78) – Hull

Blake Morrison (b.1950) – Skipton

Gervase Phinn (b.1946) - Rotherham
J.B. Priestley (1894-1967) - Bradford
Arthur Ransome (1884-1967) - Leeds
Stevie Smith (1902-71) - Hull
David Storey (b.1933) - Wakefield
Keith Waterhouse (b.1929) - Leeds

YORKSHIRE FOOD – YORKSHIRE PUDDING

Of all the foods to come out of the county, Yorkshire pudding is probably the most famous, and it sits alongside fish and chips as foreign tourists' idea of traditional English fare. Made from only flour, milk, water, eggs and seasoning, it's one of Yorkshire's simplest recipes too.

The humble pudding has become a staple of the roast Sunday lunch or dinner in Yorkshire and beyond. It was not necessarily created in Yorkshire, though the name has firmly stuck - perhaps because the county's cooks perfected a crisp, light and puffy version of it, but more likely because they have fiercely protected Yorkshire's reputation as its home. It was being referred to as Yorkshire pudding in cookery books as far back as 1747, though a similar recipe appeared as Dripping Pudding in a book with the not very forward-thinking title *The Whole Duty of a Woman* ten years earlier, and it had almost certainly been used long before that. Whenever it began, it was probably devised by frugal cooks to make the most of the juices dripping from their joint of meat as it roasted. In Yorkshire, at least, it was traditionally served before the main course - either to whet the appetite for the roast to follow or to fill people up because the expense of meat meant cooks could afford only small portions of it - though these days it is more likely to sit on the same plate alongside beef and piles of vegetables.

In Yorkshire and elsewhere the pudding has also become a meal in itself, cooked in vast, plate-sized portions and poured full of gravy, stew, chilli, curry or any number of weird and wonderful combinations. Add sausages to the mix before baking and it's toad-in-the-hole, another Yorkshire favourite. Pudding aficionados even adapt leftovers into a sweet dish, smothered in jam, syrup or ice cream. The very idea is enough to turn the stomachs of those used only to Yorkshire pudding with their roast, but its basic ingredients actually make it more of a cake or pastry than a savoury dish.

The pudding's popularity means it has been adulterated over the years, though many Yorkshire cooks would not dream of baking Yorkshire pudding in the small, muffin-sized portions that have become popular, nor of reheating the low-fat, frozen versions found in supermarkets. Because the recipe dates back so far, it also spread with British explorers and settlers across the world and has become a heart-stopping first taste of Yorkshire for many Americans in particular.

A recipe for Yorkshire pudding

80 g plain flour
1 egg
80 ml milk
60 ml water
salt and pepper
beef dripping or other cooking oil

Sift the flour into a bowl. Make a well in the centre, break the egg in and beat it. Gradually incorporate the flour around it and add the milk, water and seasoning (you can use an electric hand whisk but a fork will do) until you have a smooth batter. You may not need all the liquid. If you have time, you can do as some Yorkshire cooks advise and let the mix stand for an hour or so or even overnight. Add a tablespoon of beef dripping or other fat or oil to a medium-sized roasting tin or dish, or add a smaller amount to each compartment of a muffin tray if you're using that instead. Place in a preheated oven, 220°C (425°F), Gas Mark 7. When the dripping is sizzling hot, pour in the batter and return the tin to a high shelf for 25–30 minutes or for slightly longer on a lower shelf under your joint of beef to catch its juices, until it rises and becomes golden and crisp round the edges. Cut the pudding into portions and serve piping hot.

YORKSHIRE SAYINGS

'You can tell a Yorkshireman – but you can't tell him much.'

THE YORKSHIRE ANTHEM

Yorkshire's unofficial but widely accepted anthem is 'On Ilkley Moor Baht 'at'. The song is thought to have been composed by a Methodist church choir during a picnic outing to Ilkley Moor, and its tune follows an old hymn, 'Cranbrook'. It tells the story of a man out courting on Ilkley Moor without wearing a hat – a foolish undertaking, as anyone who has been there so dressed will appreciate. It's not exactly a cheerful anthem, since the singer goes on to imagine what will become of the man after he freezes to death on the moor.

Lyrics to the song vary, but this is a commonly used version. Each verse repeats with the line indicated, as in the first verse.

1 Wheear 'as tha bin since ah saw thee?
On Ilkley Moor baht 'at
Wheear 'as tha bin since ah saw thee?
Wheear 'as tha bin since ah saw thee?
On Ilkley Moor baht 'at,
On Ilkley Moor baht 'at,
On Ilkley Moor baht 'at.

2 Tha's bin a coortin' Mary Jane *etc.*

3 Tha's bahn t'catch thy death o' cowd *etc.*

4 Then we shall ha' to bury thee *etc.*

5 Then t'worms 'll coom an' eat thee up *etc.*

6 Then t'ducks 'll coom an' eat up t'worms *etc.*

7 Then we shall go an' eat them ducks *etc.*

8 Then we shall all 'av etten thee *etc.*

A SPOTTER'S GUIDE TO SHEEP

Yorkshire's sheep are an essential part of its landscape, shaping the hills and fields and preserving the farms, dry stone walls and enclosures of the dales and moors. Here's a guide to some of the more common breeds found across Yorkshire. Not all of them are unique to the county, but all are important to its economy and identity. They are also all featured on the priority list of the Sheep Trust, set up to help protect and promote heritage breeds that are distinctive of regions throughout the UK.

Blackface. One of the most common sheep in the country, found in different cross-breed types from region to region. They have black or black-and-white faces and legs, white fleeces and are always horned. Adaptable.

Blue Faced Leicester. One of the longest and largest breeds in the country, and also one of the best for wool, with consequently high prices. They have long, neat ears, no horns and, as the name suggests, heads that appear to have a blue tinge.

Dalesbred. A hardy breed that is native to the Dales, though it has spread far beyond and has become very popular for cross-breeding. They have black faces, with distinctive white patches above the nostrils, and round horns.

Derbyshire Gritstone. One of the country's oldest sheep breeds that has spread beyond its home county to the Yorkshire Pennines and elsewhere. With coarse, protective fleeces they are well suited to tough hillside conditions. They are large sheep with chiselled faces, black and white markings and wool-free legs.

Herdwick. Native to Cumbria rather than Yorkshire, the breed has spread to the Dales and elsewhere. It's the toughest breed of sheep in the country, able to withstand the harshest weather on high, exposed fellsides. Herdwicks have white, docile-looking faces and plain cream or grey fleeces that are tough and weatherproof.

Lonk. A large breed of sheep, popular on the Pennines and, like the Herdwick, able to withstand harsh weather and poor grazing conditions. Lonks have mostly white faces with black patches around the nose and eyes, and neat, short, white fleeces.

Rough Fell. Another strong, resilient upland breed, farmed on the Yorkshire moors and hills for centuries. They have large bodies, mostly black heads with white noses, thick, long fleeces and white legs. Rough Fells usually make for very good lamb meat.

Swaledale. One of Yorkshire's native breeds, kept on the high moors and fells and able to cope with tough weather and scanty food supplies. Swaledales are medium sized with white muzzles, white stripes above each eye, curly, wide horns and thick, long tails. Often crossed with other breeds.

FOOTBALL CLUBS IN YORKSHIRE

In the 2007-8 season the traditional county of Yorkshire had ten teams in the four divisions of the national football league - more than any other area of the country except London. Together with their years of formation, they are:

Barnsley – 1887
Bradford City – 1903
Doncaster Rovers – 1879
Huddersfield Town – 1908
Hull City – 1904
Leeds United – 1919
Middlesbrough – 1876
Rotherham United – 1884
Sheffield United – 1889
Sheffield Wednesday – 1867

YORKSHIRE POEMS

'Composed after a Journey across the Hamilton Hills, Yorkshire' by WILLIAM WORDSWORTH

Ere we had reached the wished-for place, night fell:
We were too late at least by one dark hour,
And nothing could we see of all that power
Of prospect, whereof many thousands tell.
The western sky did recompense us well
With Grecian Temple, Minaret, and Bower;
And, in one part, a Minster with its Tower
Substantially distinct, a place for Bell
Or Clock to toll from. Many a glorious pile
Did we behold, sights that might well repay
All disappointment! and, as such, the eye
Delighted in them; but we felt, the while,
We should forget them: they are of the sky,
And from our earthly memory fade away.

YORKSHIRE'S PRIME MINISTERS

Yorkshire has produced three of Britain's 51 prime ministers since Robert Walpole became, according to common agreement, the first in the job in 1721. They are:

Charles Wentworth, Marquess of Rockingham (1730–82),
born near Rotherham; prime minister from 1765 to 1766 and
again in 1782.

Herbert Henry Asquith (1852–1928), born in Morley;
prime minister from 1908 to 1916.

Harold Wilson (1916–95), born in Cowlersley;
prime minister from 1964 to 1970 and
again from 1974 to 1976.

YORKSHIRE ON FILM

The cities and countryside of the county have lent themselves to plenty
of popular films over the years. Here are twenty of the best known films
shot at least partly in Yorkshire.

Billy Liar (1963). Filmed in Bradford.

Brassed Off (1996). Scenes shot in Barnsley, Rotherham and
Doncaster. The collieries used are at Hatfield and Grimethorpe.

Calendar Girls (2003). Various Yorkshire locations, including
Kettlewell, Burnsall, Ingleton and Settle.

Elizabeth (1998). York Minister and Bolton Castle both served for
scenes.

Fanny and Elvis (1999). Yorkshire-set romantic comedy shot in
Hebden Bridge and Ilkley Moor, among other places.

The Full Monty (1997). Filmed entirely in and around Sheffield. The
final scene was shot at the Shiregreen Working Men's Club.

Harry Potter films (2001 onwards). Goathland station in the Esk
Valley became Hogsmead station.

The History Boys (2006). Halifax and Fountains Abbey both feature.

Kes (1969). Ken Loach's classic was filmed in and around Barnsley.
The school scenes were shot at what is now Edward Sheerien School
in the town.

Little Voice (1998). Filmed in Scarborough. The nightclub scenes were shot at the Cayton Bay Holiday Camp.

Possession (2002). Whitby and Pickering stations were both used for the adaptation of A.S. Byatt's novel.

A Private Function (1984). Partly shot in Bradford and Ilkley.

The Railway Children (1970). Home scenes were filmed in Oxenhope and at the Brontë Parsonage in Haworth. The railway line used is the Keighley and Worth Valley Railway, now preserved as a steam line by volunteers.

Rita, Sue and Bob Too! (1986). Set in working-class Yorkshire and filmed in Bradford, Halifax, Haworth and Baildon.

Robin Hood: Prince of Thieves (1991). Some outdoor scenes were shot at Aysgarth Falls and Hardraw Force in north Yorkshire.

The Secret Garden (1996). Fountains Abbey provided the garden.

This Sporting Life (1963). Filmed in Wakefield, Halifax and Bolton Abbey.

Up 'n' Under (1998). Set in west Yorkshire but mostly filmed in Cardiff, though some scenes were shot around Skidby Mill.

Wuthering Heights (1993). Various locations, including Keighley, Aysgarth Falls, Skipton, Malham and Halifax.

Yanks (1979). Used the Keighley and Worth Valley Railway.

THE TOP TOURIST ATTRACTIONS

Flamingoland bills itself as the UK's only theme park, zoo and holiday village. Its unique formula is obviously a successful one, as it was Yorkshire's most popular paid-for tourist attraction by some distance in 2006, attracting more than 1.3 million people through the gates to its 375 acres (152 ha) of land near Malton. Yorkshire's top free attraction in the year was Castleford's massive Xscape entertainment park, though activities here have to be paid for. The attractions in second place on both lists are within a few hundred yards of each other in York: York Minister and the National Railway Museum.

These lists and figures are collated by Yorkshire Tourist Board and need to be treated with some care as they include only places that publish their visitor figures, and some numbers are estimates only. The top ten paid-for attractions are:

Attraction	Visitors in 2006
1 Flamingo Land Theme Park and Zoo, Malton	1,302,195
2 York Minster	895,000
3 Fountains Abbey and Studley Royal Water Garden	313,388
4 Eureka! Museum, Halifax	250,364
5 Cannon Hall Open Farm, Cawthorne	250,000
6 Harewood House	221,880
7 Castle Howard	203,932
8 RHS Garden Harlow Carr, Harrogate	193,889
9 Sewerby Hall and Gardens, Bridlington	175,000
10 Magna Science Adventure Centre, Rotherham	155,210

And the top ten free attractions are:

Attraction	Visitors in 2006
1 Xscape, Castleford	3,476,000
2 National Railway Museum, York	902,149
3 Rother Valley Country Park	827,474
4 The Trans Pennine Trail	700,766
5 National Media Museum, Bradford	663,444
6 Thrybergh Country Park	350,000
7 Royal Armouries Museum, Leeds	290,098
8 Leeds City Art Gallery	286,059
9 National Coal Mining Museum, Wakefield	127,500
10 Priory Church of St Mary and St Cuthbert, Bolton Abbey	119,340

A CALENDAR OF UNUSUAL YORKSHIRE CUSTOMS

Part 1 : Spring and Summer

England is steeped in folklore festivals and celebrations that continue year in and year out, but Yorkshire seems to have more than its fair share. This is a selection of some of the most interesting annual traditions, some of them dating back centuries.

Midgley's Pace-Egg Play
Easter Sunday

An Easter version of the mummers' plays, performed by the children of the Calder Valley High School since the 1930s.

Barwick-in-Elmet's Maypole
Easter Monday and Spring Bank Holiday

Plenty of villages have maypoles but few are as tall as Barwick's at 86 feet (26 m). Every three years on Easter Monday the pole is removed by local men, repainted and garlanded before being put up again a few weeks later amid great celebration.

Gawthorpe's World Coal Carrying Championships
Easter Monday

In which strong men compete for the title of world's greatest coal carrier by carrying 50 kg sacks of coal for about two-thirds of a mile (1 km) to the maypole on the village green. The record time is around four minutes. Gawthorpe used to be coal mining territory, and the tradition was started by a bet in a pub in 1963. Women and children now have their own races too.

Helpin's Passing the Penny
Second Monday after Easter

A tradition begun by John Marsden, a local boy made good through hard work and self-education. His will stipulated that all boys of the village of 13 years or older should be given a penny to help further themselves. It continues, though since inflation has rather reduced the value of the bequest, boys now receive 'penny biscuits' instead.

Marsden's Cuckoo Day
Late April

Annual celebration to mark the return of the cuckoo. Activities include a cuckoo walk, processions and music. Legend has it that Marsden residents used to try to keep the cuckoo from leaving each year by building a wall and cursed themselves for not raising it high enough when the bird flew off.

Whitby's Planting the Penny Hedge
Saturday before Ascension Sunday

After three men killed a hermit in 1159 they were ordered as a penance to build a hedge of stocks and branches strong enough to withstand three tides on the shore at Whitby. What was Penance Hedge has become Penny Hedge, and the tradition is still observed by locals as crowds watch. Once complete, one man bellows 'Out on ye!' meaning 'Shame on You'.

The Scorton Silver Arrow
Mid-May

Ambitiously billed as the world's longest running organised sporting event. Having first met in 1673, the members of the Society of Archers continue to get together in a different Yorkshire venue each May for serious archery competitions in between some traditional customs and feasts. The Silver Arrow goes to the first archer to hit a 3 inch (8 cm) bull's eye from 100 yards (90 m) away.

Market Weighton's Giant Bradley Day
Last Sunday in May

Family-focused annual celebrations to remember the town's most famous son, William Bradley, who at 7 feet 9 inches (2.36 m) was Britain's tallest ever man. Modern-day giants are among those who attend.

The Hepworth Feast
Last Monday in June

Marks the end of the plague that decimated the west Yorkshire village in 1665. These days it's more of a fete than a feast, with processions, bands and morris dancing.

Oxenhope's Straw Race
First or second Sunday in July

Competitors must carry a bale of straw around five pubs on a 2½ mile (4 km) route, drinking a pint in each. There are prizes for the best costumes as well as the fastest runners. The custom began in the 1970s after a drunken bet but has become a major draw for visitors and a large fundraising event.

The Kilburn Feast
First Sunday after 7 July

In which a local couple dress up as a mayor and his wife before being pulled through the village in a handcart to fine people for spurious misdemeanours. The money raised goes towards a feast for the village.

Ripon's St Wilfrid's Feast Procession
Saturday before first Monday in August

St Wilfrid was an abbot of Ripon, and his return from exile to the city is celebrated with a procession to the cathedral led by a man dressed as him on a white horse, followed by a service and various celebrations.

Saddleworth's Rush Cart Ceremony
Second weekend after 12 August

Thousands of bundles of reeds are piled on 15 feet (4.6 m) high carts, pulled by morris dancers up a steep hill to the church for blessing. The tradition remembers the Saddleworth Wakes, the annual holiday of local mill and factory workers, and was revived in the 1970s.

West Witton's Burning the Bartle
Saturday nearest St Bartholomew's Day (24 August)

Locals carry a large effigy called Bartle around the village before burning it. The identity of Bartle is uncertain, though it may be St Bartholomew, a statue of whom was seized from the village during Henry VIII's dissolution. Burning the effigy seems rather disrespectful to a saint, so some have argued that Bartle was a local criminal – or it may have been done simply as a ritual ahead of harvest time.

THE STAR RESTAURANTS

Yorkshire has four restaurants with a prestigious one star rating from international assessor Michelin. They are:

The Star Inn, Harome, near Helmsley
Tel. 01439 770397 or visit www.thestaratharome.co.uk

The Box Tree, Ilkley
Tel. 01943 608484 or visit www.theboxtree.co.uk

The Yorke Arms, Ramsgill-in-Nidderdale, near Pateley Bridge
Tel. 01423 755423 or visit www.yorke-arms.co.uk

The Old Vicarage, Sheffield
Tel. 01142 475814 or visit www.theoldvicarage.co.uk

Ten more places received a Bib Gourmand from Michelin inspectors for 'good food at moderate prices'. They are:

The Dining Room, Boroughbridge
The General Tarleton Inn, Ferrensby
The Angel Inn, Hetton
Anthony's at Flannels, Leeds
Brasserie Forty Four, Leeds
Vennell's, Masham
Artisan, Sheffield
The Millbank, Sowerby Bridge
The Rose and Crown, Sutton-on-the-Forest
J. Baker's, York

YORKSHIRE'S LAZIEST WORKING MEN

Don't worry, residents of the Yorkshire village of Idle have heard most of the jokes before. And those who do their socializing and drinking on the High Street attract the most teasing of all, since they are members of one of the best named societies in England: The Idle Working Men's Club.

There's no reason to think that the working men here, just north of Bradford, are any lazier than their fellow Yorkshiremen, of course - and the committee of the club probably works harder than most, since they field endless enquiries and lame jokes from amused visitors. Many of the requests they receive are for affiliate membership, from people eager for a card to prove their accreditation as Idle Working Men, and the club patiently puts up with people stopping to have their photo taken outside the building.

The club has encouraged the joke with a logo of a flat-capped man resting on his shovel, and it does decent business in a line of souvenir clothing. It now has more than 1,300 members in all corners of the world, including celebrities like jockey Lester Piggott, actor Roger Moore, footballer Paul Gascoigne and - rather incongruously - singer Michael Jackson. Details of how to join them can be found at www.vvg-studio.co.uk/idle.The club opens every night and was one of the first of its kind to admit female members, a move that means it remains an important and busy part of the community. Rumours of a partnership with the Women's Institute in the Kent town of Loose are unconfirmed. But while many working men's clubs across the country struggle to compete with alternative entertainments, this is one that is in no danger of falling idle.

THE SOUND OF YORKSHIRE

They're not exclusive to Yorkshire, of course, but brass bands are undoubtedly the musical sound most commonly associated with the county.

In some ways, the tradition of the brass bands is also the recent story of Yorkshire. Many of the original bands were drawn from the mines, mills, factories and military of Yorkshire, and the enthusiasm with which they developed reflected huge local pride in the workplace and community. Made up of cornets, tubas, trombones, tenor horns, flugelhorns and other instruments, bands would often spring up in small mining towns and villages, where there was less entertainment than in the cities and where communities were tighter. Initially playing for their own families and friends in local halls, as their popularity spread bands would begin to tour other local venues. Competition started to intensify, between or even within industries and towns.

Just as brass bands rose with Yorkshire's booming industries, so they declined with their fall. But while some have wound up, particularly after the government's pit closures programme, others have continued, and newer sponsors have emerged to support them, including the likes of the Yorkshire Building Society and the Co-op. Band members these days are drawn from further afield than was the case in the past, but interest in the bands and their performances is still strong. The brass band community is well organised, and rivalries culminate in the National Brass Band Championships. Within Yorkshire, the Yorkshire and Humberside Brass Band Association oversees dozens of members, and competitions include an annual festival on Hardraw Scar, where the natural amphitheatre provides a beautiful backdrop and perfect acoustics for the sound of the brass bands.

Bands' associations with the now-closed collieries of Yorkshire are particularly poignant, giving their warm sound a somewhat melancholy aspect. The links were explored in the popular 1996 film *Brassed Off*, the story of a fictional south Yorkshire band at the time of the pit closures. It was based on the experiences of the Grimethorpe Colliery band, which provided the film's soundtrack and which has been touring on the back of it ever since.

BERNARD INGHAM'S FIFTY GREATEST YORKSHIRE PEOPLE

It's a brave man who tries to make a list of Yorkshire's greatest people, risking the ire of those he has left out and their supporters. But Sir Bernard Ingham – formerly Margaret Thatcher's press secretary and latterly a prolific writer and broadcaster – made a pretty good stab of it in his book *Yorkshire Greats* (Dalesman). Whittled down from the thousand or so Yorkshire men and women in the *Dictionary of National Biography*, his list mixes people from all fields of endeavour and – apart from singling out a top trio of James Cook, William Wilberforce and John Harrison – is not ranked in any order. It includes only six living people, and – to much consternation – only five women. Ingham's fifty Yorkshire greats, in order of birth, are:

Edwin (585-633), saint
Alcuin (732-804), scholar
John Wycliffe (1330-84), theologian
John Fisher (1469-1535), saint
Henry Briggs (1561-1630), mathematician
Guy Fawkes (1570-1606), Gunpowder Plot conspirator
William Bradford (1590-1657), pilgrim father
Thomas Fairfax (1612-71), soldier
Andrew Marvell (1621-78), poet
John Harrison (1693-1776), clockmaker
Thomas Chippendale (1718-79), furniture maker
John Smeaton (1724-92), engineer
James Cook (1728-79), explorer
Charles Wentworth (1730-82), prime minister
Joseph Priestley (1733-1804), scientist
Joseph Bramah (1748-1814), inventor
William Wilberforce (1759-1833), campaigner and abolitionist
George Cayley (1773-1857), aeronautical engineer
Titus Salt (1803-76), industrialist
John Curwen (1816-80), musician
Emily Brontë (1818-48), writer
Augustus Pitt-Rivers (1827-1900), anthropologist
Herbert Asquith (1852-1928), prime minister
Michael Sadler (1861-1943), educationalist
William Bateson (1861-1926), geneticist
Almroth Wright (1861-1947), bacteriologist
Frederick Delius (1862-1934), composer
William Congreve (1670-1729), playwright
Harry Brearley (1871-1948), inventor
J. Arthur Rank (1888-1972), film producer
Percy Shaw (1890-1976), inventor
J.B. Priestley (1894-1984), writer
John Cockroft (1897-1967), scientist
Henry Moore (1898-1986), sculptor
Charles Laughton (1899-1962), actor

Amy Johnson (1903–41), aviator

Stanley Hollis (1912–72), soldier and Victoria Cross holder

Fred Hoyle (1915–2001), astronomer

Harold Wilson (1916–95), prime minister

Len Hutton (1916–90), cricketer

Betty Boothroyd (b.1929), politician

Ted Hughes (1930–98), poet

Fred Trueman (1931–2006), cricketer

Janet Baker (b.1933), singer

John Barry (b.1933), composer

Alan Bennett (b.1934), writer

Brian Clough (1935–2004), football player and manager

David Hockney (b.1937), artist

Barbara Harrison (1945–68), air stewardess and
George Cross medal holder

Alan Hinkes (b.1954), mountaineer

BIBLICAL PROPORTIONS

Yorkshire is by some distance England's biggest county, and proud residents are fond of saying it has more acres than the bible has letters. Unlike some Yorkshire sayings, this one's true: measured to its historic borders, Yorkshire has some 3.8 million acres, edging out the 3.6 million letters in the Old and New Testaments.

THE CHARACTERISTICS OF A 19TH-CENTURY YORKSHIREMAN

In 1892 the Reverend M.C.F. Morris of Newton-on-Ouse near York published his snappily titled *Yorkshire Folk-Talk with Characteristics of Those Who Speak It in the North and East Ridings*. It contained some fairly forthright opinions on the good and bad aspects of the Yorkshire character, many of them gathered from his circle of friends from outside the county. Judge for yourself how much Yorkshire people have changed since the good reverend made his observations.

On manners
'Nearly all Southerners agree that our manners are not good. We are supposed to be rough and rude ... The Yorkshireman has, no doubt, a way of speaking his mind very freely, and telling you what he thinks. However unpleasant this habit may be at times, it has its advantages; you at least know where you are with them and you can always tell whether a Yorkshireman likes or dislikes what you do – he as good as tells you.'

On attitudes to money
'Outsiders say "Yorkshiremen are such money-lovers" or "They keep such a tight grip over their purses" or "It is uncommonly hard to get any money out of them." Well, I daresay it is true that we, like a great many others, know the value of money fairly well. Perhaps even we attach a greater value to such a small sum as twopence than the Londoner does; still for all that, the Yorkshireman can be, and is, most liberal with his money when the reason for laying it out seems to him clearly to be a strong and a valid one.'

On unfussy outlooks
'A more practical people do not exist than Yorkshire people. They look at everything from a practical point of view. What is best to be done under the circumstances is a question which they know well how to answer in effect at all times.'

On a wariness of outsiders
'It is true they are suspicious and shy of strangers, but whenever they admit another to their confidence, they are the truest and most steadfast of friends ... [But] I should give a very incomplete account of the Yorkshireman's character if I did not say that he is hospitable; in this respect at all events he is seldom found wanting. If you enter a Yorkshireman's house, he is ever ready to welcome you to his table and to offer you the best he has; this excellent quality pervades all classes alike.'

On musical abilities
'It is generally supposed that Yorkshire people are musical. This is a statement which requires considerable qualification. Yorkshire is a large area, and there are parts of the county of which it certainly cannot be said that the people are musical ... I cannot help thinking however that a hilly country is distinctly more favourable to vocal power than a flat country, and good air, of course, than bad air.'

On loyalty to Yorkshire
'Their ideas of geography and history are, as one might imagine, amusingly vague; but they know every inch of their own country, and treasure the biographies of their own kin.'

FAMOUS YORKSHIRE FOLK – JOHN HARRISON

Although it can only really claim him by birth, that's good enough for Yorkshire to consider John Harrison one of its own.

The man who revolutionised sea travel by solving the problem of how to keep true time and work out longitude was born in Foulby, between Wakefield and Pontefract, in 1693, but he moved with his family to Lincolnshire at seven. After a few years as an apprentice in his father's carpentry trade, Harrison devoted virtually his whole life to the riddle of longitude, and despite endless challenges to his reputation in his own lifetime, he is now widely accepted as the father of the marine chronometer.

Unlike many pioneers of his time, Harrison was born into a family of relatively modest means and achieved what he did through natural intelligence and hard work rather than education and money. He started with wooden clocks but was soon building devices that didn't lose time from friction or corrosion in parts, from rough movements or from changes in temperature – all common problems at sea. As he did so, the government put up a prize of £20,000 – several million pounds in modern value – for anyone who could produce a method of determining longitude with precision, and Harrison tackled the challenge full on. By 1735 he had created a chronometer that proved extremely accurate after a test voyage, and after 25 more years of fine-tuning he produced a large watch that after two trips to the Caribbean and back was found to have kept time to within a couple of minutes.

Though his achievements might seem rather rudimentary by modern, hi-tech standards, they came at a time when sea travel – both to explore the world and to trade – was rapidly increasing, and it is difficult to overestimate Harrison's effect. Calculating 'true' time allowed sailors accurately to assess longitude and hence their precise location in the world and so reduce the risk of getting lost or shipwrecked.

Harrison had to put up with opposition from those who distrusted his methods and thought that an accurate, portable chronometer such as his was impossible. Astronomers were particularly frosty, irate that a mere mechanic like Harrison should solve the problem ahead of them. It took years of wrangling for Harrison to get even some of the prize money he was entitled to, and he died in 1776, soon after finally receiving it. Though it took more time for his invention to be properly adapted for mass production, by the start of the 19th century it was a common tool on board ships around the world, saving lives and making the world a much smaller place.

YORKSHIRE'S MOST AND LEAST WANTED POSTCODES

Ilkley and Wetherby are the most expensive towns for property in the Yorkshire and Humber region, while Hull and Scunthorpe are the cheapest places to find a house. These top tens are arranged by postal town and ranked according to the 2007 Halifax House Price Index, which monitors average selling prices and properties across the country.

Most expensive	**Least expensive**
1 Ilkley	1 Hull
2 Wetherby	2 Scunthorpe
3 Harrogate	3 Barnsley
4 York	4 Dewsbury
5 Skipton	5 Grimsby
6 Otley	6 Bradford
7 Whitby	7 Batley
8 Northallerton	8 Cleethorpes
9 Bingley	9 Halifax
10 Driffield	10 Rotherham

THE HIGHEST MOUNTAINS

Separating and ranking mountains is a tricky business. Is a peak a mountain in its own right or merely part of a next-door neighbour? It's doubly hard when it comes to Yorkshire and its shifting boundaries over the years. This ranking is based on the popular and widely respected 'Nuttalls' classification – which defines a mountain as being over 2,000 feet (610 m) high with a rise on all sides from its immediate surroundings of at least 50 feet (15 m) – and takes as its limits the boundaries of the historic county of Yorkshire rather than the modern administrative areas.

The top 20 tops that result are mostly in the Yorkshire Dales, except the highest one of all, Mickle Fell. This is in the north Pennines, inside the historic borders of Yorkshire by a matter of yards and now – after the county boundary shake-up – part of Durham. If you make a more modern interpretation of Yorkshire's boundaries – as many walkers like to do – then the highest point is Whernside, in the Dales. But while Yorkshire is a hilly place by most standards, its tops are dwarfed by the Lake District, which has 44 mountains higher than Mickle Fell and 74 higher than Whernside.

		Height	
		in feet	in metres
1	Mickle Fell	2,585	788
2	Whernside	2,415	736
3	Ingleborough	2,372	723
4	Great Shunner Fell	2,349	716
5	High Seat	2,326	709
6	Wild Boar Fell	2,323	708
7	Great Whernside	2,310	704
8	Buckden Pike	2,303	702
9	Archy Styrigg (also known as Gregory Chapel)	2,280	695
10	Pen-y-Ghent	2,277	694
11	Hugh Seat	2,260	689
12	Great Coum	2,254	687
13	Swarth Fell	2,234	681
14	Plover Hill	2,231	680
15	Baugh Fell (also known as Tarn Rigg Hill)	2,224	678
16=	The Calf	2,218	676
16=	Knoutberry Haw	2,218	676
18	Lovely Seat	2,215	675
19	Calders	2,211	674
20=	Bram Rigg Top	2,205	672
20=	Great Knoutberry Hill	2,205	672
20=	Rogan's Seat	2,205	672

A BRIEF HISTORY OF THE WHITE ROSE

The white rose is traditionally supposed to represent purity and innocence – but to Yorkshire folk it always means home.

There have been disagreements about the point at which the white rose properly became Yorkshire's official emblem, but it was probably used for the first time by the first Duke of York, Edmund, in the 14th century. The rose was then adopted by York men as one of the emblems of the area in the 15th-century battles with the House of Lancaster, whose men took the red rose as their symbol. Soldiers used many other emblems of their various lords and masters, of course, and the roses were far from being the official logos of the two sides. But when Henry VII ended the last phase of battles in 1485, he made a symbolic gesture of uniting the two roses into a single red and white flower, the Tudor Rose.

The fierce civil wars only became popularly known as the Wars of the Roses a few centuries later, but by that time the powerful resonance of the white rose in Yorkshire had been firmly established. Shakespeare refers to the white rose in *Henry VI*, written in the 1580s and 1590s. And on 1 August 1759 soldiers from Yorkshire regiments at the Battle of Minden picked white roses in tribute to their fallen colleagues. This date has since been adopted as Yorkshire Day, when all Yorkshire people are encouraged to wear the white rose, and some people argue that it was in this battle rather than during the Wars of the Roses that the flower properly became Yorkshire's emblem. Whether the roses were picked by the soldiers for their emblematic value or simply because they happened to be nearby is unclear.

Either way, the white rose has become a widely used and cherished symbol of Yorkshire, and its importance is such that there have been serious arguments about which way up the popular five-petalled depiction of it should be arranged. Cricket matches between Yorkshire and Lancashire – and indeed just about any sporting fixture between teams from the two counties – are still known as Roses games, and the flower has been adopted as an emblem by a host of Yorkshire organisations and businesses. Leeds even has a White Rose Shopping Centre – perhaps not exactly what the soldiers of the Wars of the Roses and the Battle of Minden had in mind all those years ago, but proof of the power of the emblem.

AROUND THE WORLD IN DRY STONE WALLS

Dry stone walls are a distinctive part of the Yorkshire landscape, and this part of the country has more of them than any other. According to a survey by the Countryside Agency, Yorkshire has around 18,900 miles (30,420 km) of dry stone walls, more than a quarter of England's total of 70,400 miles (112,600 km). Put end to end, Yorkshire's dry stone walls would be long enough to:

Reach from Leeds to Alice Springs in the heart of Australia
Enclose the whole of Britain by running around the entire coastline
Link John o'Groats to Land's End more than 20 times
Encircle London 162 times by stretching around the M25
Stretch three-quarters of the way around the earth's equator

WHO ATE ALL THE PIES?

Yorkshire has always loved its pies, and there is fierce competition between makers and towns about who bakes the best. But there is no doubt who makes the biggest.

Denby Dale near Huddersfield has been the proud – and perhaps only – baker of giant pies for more than 200 years. The tradition began with a pie baked to celebrate the recovery from mental illness of King George III in 1788 and has continued every couple of decades since, either to mark significant national events or to raise money for local causes. The pies have got bigger at each baking, the tin increasing in diameter from 16 feet (4.8 m) in 1928 to 40 feet (12 m) in 2000. That millennium pie weighed some 12 tons and contained thousands of pounds of beef, potatoes and onions. One of the old pie dishes can be seen outside the village hall that it helped to raise funds for, having been adapted for use as a flower planter.

Not all bakings have been entirely successful. In 1887, when villagers set about making a pie to celebrate Queen Victoria's Jubilee, something went wrong with the recipe – a minor mishap when baking a normal pie, but a bit of a calamity when it weighs a ton and a half. The pie was deemed unfit for human consumption, buried in quicklime and quickly replaced with a new 'Resurrection Pie'.

Denby Dale trades well on its heritage, with signs billing itself as the pie village and its own pie firm, the Denby Dale Pie Company. Its other claim to size fame is that it is within sight of Britain's tallest self-supporting structure, the 1,082 feet (330 m) Emley TV mast.

Pie history: Occasions marked by Denby Dale's ten pies

The recovery from mental illness of King George III, 1788

The victory of the Duke of Wellington over Napoleon
at Waterloo, 1815

The repeal of the Corn Laws, 1846

Queen Victoria's Jubilee, 1887 (two pies)

The 50th anniversary of the repeal of the Corn Laws, 1896

Fundraising for Huddersfield Royal Infirmary, 1928

The birth of royal babies, including Prince Edward, and
fundraising for a village hall, 1964

Bicentenary of the first pie, 1988

The millennium and the Queen Mother's 100th birthday, 2000

WORLD HERITAGE SITES

Along with London, Yorkshire is the only part of the country to have more than one World Heritage site.

The first to be designated as such by UNESCO, in 1986, was **Studley Royal Park**, including the historic ruins of Fountains Abbey. Founded in 1132 by a group of 13 monks who had been exiled from nearby St Mary's Abbey at York, Fountains Abbey is one of the most spectacular Cistercian sites in the country. Henry VIII's dissolution of the monasteries emptied it in 1539, but while it then fell into disrepair and was robbed of much of its stone for the building of the nearby Fountains Hall mansion, the abbey is remarkably well preserved. It is now owned by the National Trust and looked after by English Heritage, and it is open all year round (tel. 01765 608888 or visit www.fountainsabbey.org.uk).

Yorkshire's other World Heritage Site is **Saltaire** in Bradford, designated in 2001. It is a purpose-built and very well preserved industrial village, constructed in the 1850s by Sir Titus Salt to provide homes and facilities for workers at his textile mills. Salt was a rare combination of mill magnate and enlightened philanthropist, and his 'model' village on the River Aire had stone houses, running water, a hospital, library, concert hall, park and educational institute. The contrast between Saltaire and the dreadful conditions in and around the 'dark satanic mills' of Yorkshire cities like Bradford and Leeds must have been remarkable. Visit www.saltaire-village.co.uk for more information about Saltaire and the mill's new life as a creative centre.

GREAT YORKSHIRE INVENTIONS

Though Joseph Priestley and John Harrison, profiled elsewhere in this book, are undoubtedly responsible for Yorkshire's most important scientific discoveries, there have been plenty more inventors and pioneers over the centuries. Here are ten of the most interesting.

James Henry Atkinson (1849-1942), an ironmonger from Leeds, invented the classic spring-loaded **mousetrap** in the late 1890s. He called it the Little Nipper and made a decent sum from selling the rights to a manufacturer.

Donald Bailey (1901-85), born in Rotherham, invented the **Bailey Bridge**, a portable and dismantable bridge used by military units to cross rivers or gaps up to 200 feet (60 m) in length. It was especially important to Allied troops during the Second World War.

Joseph Bramah (1748-1814), born in Wentworth, invented the **hydraulic press** - still often known as the Bramah press in his honour - and, more significantly for most Yorkshiremen, the **beer pump**.

Harry Brearley (1871-1948) invented **Sheffield Steel**. Born in Sheffield, his father was a steel worker and he studied metallurgy from an early age. His discovery of a way of producing a metal that didn't rust gave new impetus to the city's steel industry.

George Cayley (1773-1857) from near Scarborough invented, among a host of other things, a series of **glider-type aircraft** through the early 19th century - decades before the Wright brothers were credited with the first manned flight.

Thomas Crapper (1836-1918), a plumber born in Thorne in south Yorkshire, was not the sole inventor of the **flushing toilet**, but he did most to advance and improve it. And his name, of course, means he will forever be associated with it.

The magnificently named Wordsworth Donisthorpe (1847-1914) of Leeds invented the **kinesigraph**, a camera that took photos at regular intervals to capture movement on film - making him one of the pioneers of cinematography.

Joseph Hansom (1803-83) of York invented the **hansom cab**. An architect by trade, his design for a two-wheeled, horse-drawn carriage mixed speed with greater safety. York's city centre has a pub called the Hansom Cab in his honour.

John Kilner (1792-1857), born in Dewsbury, invented the **kilner jar** for storing food in an airtight environment. He and his family once had several glassmaking factories around Yorkshire, though the business failed in the 1930s.

Percy Shaw (1890-1976), born in Halifax, invented **catseyes**, perhaps the most important ever road safety tool. There are several versions of how he made his discovery, but the most interesting has it that the reflection from a stray cat's eyes one night helped to keep him on the road. Production of his invention, patented in 1934, increased rapidly during the blackouts of the Second World War.

YORKSHIRE TOURISM IN NUMBERS

Some statistics about visitors to Yorkshire in 2006, compiled by the Yorkshire Tourist Board.

6,136,000,000 . . . . .value in pounds to the economy of tourism
104,600,000 . . . . .tourist trips to Yorkshire
91,800,000 . . . . .day visits
11,600,000 .overnight visits by UK residents
1,200,000 . . . . .overnight visits by overseas residents
61 . . . . . . .percentage of rooms in serviced accommodation occupied
during the year
43 . . . . . . .percentage of UK trippers staying with friends or relatives
36 . . . . .percentage of overseas trippers visiting in July, August or
September, the most popular months of the year
34 . . . . . . .percentage of UK trippers using serviced accommodation
17 . . . . .percentage of UK trippers camping or caravanning
8.5 . . . . .percentage of England's total tourist industry by value
accounted for by Yorkshire
6 . . . . . .percentage of UK trippers using self-catering accommodation
2.7 .average nights' stay by overnight visitors

TEN UNUSUAL MUSEUMS

Yorkshire has hundreds of museums, galleries and exhibitions, but not many visitors know it is home to some of the world's best collections of reed organs, trolleybuses or lunatic asylum equipment. Many of these quirky museums are staffed by enthusiastic volunteers, and while their appeal might seem limited, they can all provide a diverting hour or two.

Beside the Seaside, Bridlington. A recreation of Yorkshire seaside holidays of yesteryear - boarding house, Punch and Judy show, deckchairs and all. Tel. 01262 674308 or visit www.bridlington.net/besidetheseaside.

Ilkley Toy Museum. A journey back to childhood, whatever your age. Tel. 01943 603855 or visit www.ilkleytoymuseum.co.uk.

Last of the Summer Wine Exhibition, Holmfirth. Bits and pieces from Yorkshire's most famous TV series, partly housed in Compo's front room. Tel. 01484 681408 or visit www.wrinkledstocking.co.uk.

The National Fairground Archive. Fascinating memorabilia from travelling fairs and circuses through the years, housed by Sheffield University. Tel. 0114 222 7231 or visit www.shef.ac.uk/nfa.

The Peace Museum, Bradford. 'Building a culture of peace through a range of exhibits, lectures, theatre and film.' Tel. 01274 754009 or visit www.peacemuseum.org.uk.

The Postcard Museum, Holmfirth. Thousands and thousands of postcards, including romantic and comic collections. Tel. 01484 222430 or visit www.picturedrome.net.

The Bus Museum, Rotherham. Great museum - if you like buses. Visit www.sheffieldbusmuseum.com.

Stephen Beaumont Museum, Wakefield. Museum of an old lunatic asylum, with a padded cell and some terrifying looking equipment. Tours by arrangement. Tel. 01924 328654.

The Trolleybus Museum, Sandtoft, Doncaster. If you like the Bus Museum you'll probably enjoy this too. Tel. 01724 711391 or visit www.sandtoft.org.

The Victorian Reed Organ and Harmonium Museum, Saltaire. A private passion that became a museum. Tel. 01274 585601.

THE YORKSHIRE TOAST

'Here's tiv us, all on us, an' me an' all
May wa nivver want nowt, none o' us,
Nor me nawther.'

YORKSHIRE'S BREWERIES

Yorkshire has a long heritage of brewing, but the beer business has never been in finer health than it is now. Thanks to surging interest in real ale and some tax breaks from the government for small breweries, there are now 70 or so places producing beer for Yorkshire and beyond. From tiny operations at the back of pubs to vast global empires like Tetley's or John Smith's, there is a vast range of brews for drinkers to choose from. Some breweries now produce bottled beers that are available across the country, and some offer tours of their premises for anyone interested in finding out more about the process and tasting a drop or two. As demand increases, more little companies are springing up every year. Here are Yorkshire's breweries:

Abbey Bells, Selby
Abbeydale Brewery, Sheffield
Acorn Brewery, Barnsley
Anglo-Dutch Brewery, Dewsbury
Atlas Mill Brewery, Brighouse
Bare Arts Brewery, Todmorden
Black Dog Brewery, Whitby
Black Sheep Brewery, Masham
Bob's Brewing Company, Ossett
Bradfield Brewery, Bradfield
Bridestones Brewing Company,
   Hebden Bridge
Briscoe's Brewery, Otley
Brown Cow Brewery, Selby
Captain Cook Brewery, Stokesley
Clark's Brewery, Wakefield
Concertina Brewery,
   Mexborough
Copper Dragon Brewery, Skipton
Cropton Brewery, Cropton
Crown Brewery, Sheffield
Daleside Brewery, Harrogate
Elland Brewery, Elland
Empire Brewery, Huddersfield
Fernandes Brewery, Wakefield
Four Alls Brewery, Ovington
Fox and Newt, Leeds
Garton Brewery, Driffield
Glentworth Brewery, Doncaster
Golcar Brewery, Huddersfield
Goose Eye Brewery, Keighley
Great Newsome Brewery, Hull
Greenfield Brewery, Saddleworth
Halifax Steam Brewing Company,
   Halifax
Hambleton Ales, Melmerby
John Smith's Brewery, Tadcaster
Joshua Tetley & Son, Leeds
Kelham Island Brewery, Sheffield
Leeds Brewery, Leeds

Linfit Brewery, Huddersfield
Little Valley Brewery,
   Hebden Bridge
Litton Ale Brewery, Skipton
Naylor's Brewery, Crosshills
North Yorkshire Brewing
   Company, Guisborough
Oakwell Brewery, Barnsley
Old Bear Brewery, Keighley
Old Mill Brewery, Snaith
Old Spot Brewery, Bradford
Ossett Brewery, Ossett
Roosters Brewing Company,
   Knaresborough
Rudgate Brewery, Tockwith
Ryburn Brewery, Sowerby Bridge
Saddleworth Brewery,
   Saddleworth
Salamander Brewing, Bradford
Saltaire Brewery, Bradford
Samuel Smith, Tadcaster
Sheffield Brewery, Sheffield
Summer Wine Brewery,
   Holmfirth
Theakston, Masham
Three Peaks Brewery, Settle
Tigertops Brewery, Wakefield
Timothy Taylor, Keighley
Turkey Inn Brewery, Oakworth
Wensleydale Brewery, Leyburn
Wentworth Brewery, Rotherham
WF6 Brewing Company,
   Normanton
Whalebone Brewery, Hull
Wharfedale Brewery, Rylstone
Wold Top Brewery, Driffield
York Brewery Company, York
Yorkshire Dales Brewing
   Company, Leyburn

SOME TWIN TOWNS

What do Freetown in Sierra Leone, Anchorage in Alaska and Esteli in Nicaragua all have in common? Not a lot - except they are all twin cities or towns of places in Yorkshire.

They are among a host of unlikely links that local authorities say help to keep Yorkshire on the map internationally - as well as providing council officials with the excuse for a few exotic foreign jaunts. Many Yorkshire towns have links with places of similar size in France or Germany, but others have been a bit more ambitious in their twinning, seeking out partners as far north as Alaska and as far south as the Falkland Islands. In keeping with its industrial heritage, many of the newer twinning arrangements have been with the new manufacturing powerhouses of China and eastern Europe.

This is not an exhaustive list, and towns may have more twinning arrangements than are listed, but these are some of Yorkshire's more interesting twins or partners.

Town	Twin
Barnsley	Gorlovka, Ukraine
Bradford	Galway, Ireland; Skopje, Macedonia
Calderdale	Musoma, Tanzania; County Mayo, Ireland
Doncaster	Wilmington, Delaware, USA; Dandong, China; Gliwice, Poland
Halifax	Halifax, Nova Scotia, Canada
Haworth	Haworth, New Jersey, USA
Hull	Freetown, Sierra Leone
Keighley	Myrtle Beach, South Carolina, USA
Kirklees	Kostanai, Kazakhstan
Leeds	Durban, South Africa; Hangzhou, China; Louisville, Kentucky, USA; Colombo, Sri Lanka
Middlesbrough	Masvingo, Zimbabwe; Middlesboro, Kentucky, USA; Dunkirk, France
Richmond	Nord Fron, Norway
Sheffield	Esteli, Nicaragua; Anshan, China; Donetsk, Ukraine
Wakefield	Belgorod, Russia; Konin, Poland
Whitby	Anchorage, Alaska; Cooktown, Australia; Nuku'Alofa, Tonga; Stanley, Falkland Islands
York	Dijon, France

YORKSHIRE FARMING

As it has in the rest of the country, farming in Yorkshire has changed dramatically over the last 50 years or so. The pressure on prices has pushed many farms out of business, and the 2001 foot and mouth disease crisis put paid to more, particularly smaller holdings. In line with the rest of the country, the number of people working on farms in Yorkshire has declined by a quarter to a third over the last couple of decades.

Though it caused terrible trauma in Yorkshire, the foot and mouth outbreak did at least force many farms to think about diversification and alternative sources of income. Many Yorkshire farms now offer accommodation or take their produce direct to consumers via farmers' markets or farm shops, and while some continue to struggle, others are thriving. One of the best places to learn more about farming in the county over the centuries is at the Yorkshire Museum of Farming, just outside York at Murton Park (tel. 01904 489966 or visit www.murtonpark.co.uk).

These farming facts and figures are based on the Yorkshire and Humber region, as defined by the 2006 agricultural and horticultural survey by the Department for Environment, Food and Rural Affairs (Defra).

4,237 . . . . .square miles (19,973 sq km) of farmed land
21,599 . . . . . .farm holdings in Yorkshire (a holding is defined as land
farmed in one unit, and farms can have more than one holding)
5,118 . . . . .grazing livestock farm holdings
2,987 . . . . .cereal farm holdings
1,434 . . . . .general cropping farm holdings
1,156 . . . . .dairy farm holdings
771 . . . . .poultry farm holdings
413 . . . . .pig farm holdings
8,757 . . . . .farm holdings under 12.3 acres (5 ha) in size
3,257 . . . . .farm holdings more than 247 acres (100 ha) in size
11,837 . . . . .full-time farmers and spouses
38,513 . . . . .total farm labour
18,673 . . . . .average net annual income in pounds per farm in
the northeast

Livestock held by farms
13,982,439 . . . . .chickens
2,182,891 . . . . .sheep
1,334,973 . . . . .pigs

553,032	.cattle
427,787	.ducks
16,449	.geese
12,661	.goats

YORKSHIRE'S CITIES

Of England's 50 places that can call themselves cities, Yorkshire has seven. A city is usually thought to be defined as a large town with a cathedral, but the status is actually only conferred by royal charter. Yorkshire's cities, in order of their year of official incorporation, are:

York - predates historical records
Leeds - 1207
Hull - 1299
Ripon - 1836
Wakefield - 1888
Sheffield - 1893
Bradford - 1897

WINNERS OF THE YORKSHIRE AWARDS

The Yorkshire Awards were set up in the late 1980s to honour those who have made important contributions to life in the county. Anyone can submit nominations, from which a judging committee picks winners in various categories. Previous recipients in four of the top awards are as follows.

	Man of the Year	Woman of the Year
2007	John Sentamu, Archbishop of York	Diane Thompson, businesswoman
2006	David Jones, businessman	Jane Tomlinson, fundraiser
2005	Alan Hinkes, mountaineer	Kay Mellor, actress
2004	Graham Kirkham, businessman	Jane Tomlinson, fundraiser
2003	Richard Whiteley, TV presenter	Nell McAndrew, TV personality
2002	Sean Bean, actor	Linda Barker, TV personality
2001	Patrick Stewart, actor	Kathy Staff, actress
2000	Michael Palin, TV personality	Lesley Garrett, opera singer

Year		
1999	Kevin Keegan, footballer	Prunella Scales, actress
1998	Michael Parkinson, TV personality	Jane McDonald, TV personality
1997	Alan Titchmarsh, TV personality	Judith Donovan, businesswoman
1996	Harold 'Dickie' Bird, cricket umpire	Liz Dawn, actress
1995	Marcus Fox, politician	Rita Britton, fashion designer
1994	Alan Ayckbourn, playwright	Jan Fletcher, businesswoman
1993	Denis Healey, politician	Elizabeth Peacock, politician
1992	Jimmy Saville, TV personality	Betty Boothroyd, politician
1991	Merlyn Rees, politician	Jean Rook, journalist
1990	Duncan Walker, cardiac surgeon	Marti Caine, singer and comedian
1989	Peter Elliott, athlete	HRH Duchess of Kent

Year	**Arts**	**Sporting**
2007	G.P. Taylor, author	Adil Rashid, cricketer
2006	Chris Moyles, radio presenter	Neil Warnock, football manager
2005	Alan Ayckbourn, playwright	Michael Vaughan and Matthew Hoggard, cricketers
2004	Clare Teal, singer	Jason Robinson and Mike Tindall, rugby union players
2003	Bill Maynard, actor	Michael Vaughan, cricketer
2002	Jude Kelly, artistic director	David Byas, cricketer
2001	Gaynor Faye, actress	Kevin Darley, jockey
2000	John Godber, playwright	Dougie Lampkin, motorcylist
1999	Keith Waterhouse and Willis Hall, writers	Jonathan Woodgate, footballer
1998	Kay Mellor, actress	Sheffield Eagles, rugby league club
1997	Roy Clarke, TV writer	Danny Wilson, football manager
1996	Ashley Jackson, artist	David Seaman, footballer
1995	Jude Kelly, artistic director	Garry Schofield, rugby league player
1994	Roy Castle, TV personality	Darren Gough, cricketer
1993	Nicholas Page, actor	Mick Hill, javelin thrower

ENGLAND'S OLDEST VILLAGE

Though one or two other places lay claim to the title, Rudston is usually acknowledged as the oldest inhabited village in England.

Lying 6 miles (10 km) inland from the east coast town of Bridlington, there is evidence of people living at Rudston as far back as Neolithic times - roughly between 8000 and 5000 BC. One of the most obvious clues to ancient inhabitation is the monolith next to the village church. At about 26 feet (8 m) high and 6 feet (1.8 m) wide, and weighing about 40 tons, this Bronze Age carved monolith is the tallest standing stone in the country. Stone for it was probably brought from the coast, and it may have supported a cross at one time. The Old English words *rood* and *stan*, meaning cross and stone, give the village of Rudston its name.

There are several other Neolithic and Bronze Age burial sites around the village, and excavations in the 1930s also uncovered a villa dating from the time of the Roman occupation. Pieces of the villa's mosaic pavement are now on display at the Hull and East Riding Museum in Hull. Rudston's church was probably built around the monolith in the early 12th century.

Rudston now has a population of around 400 people. Another of its claims to fame is that novelist Winifred Holtby is buried in the churchyard.

YORKSHIRE'S CRICKET RECORDS

Some of the most important team and individual first-class achievements since Yorkshire played their first official game in 1863. All records as at the start of the 2008 season.

38,558 . . . . .Most runs in a Yorkshire career, by Herbert Sutcliffe

3,597 . . . . .Most wickets in a Yorkshire career, by Wilfred Rhodes

2,883 . . . . .Most runs in a season, by Herbert Sutcliffe in 1932

1,665 . . . . .Most runs in a single match, vs. Warwickshire in 2002

887 . . . . .Highest team score, vs. Warwickshire in 1896

681 for 7 . . . . . . .Highest opposition score, by Leicestershire in 1996

555 . . . . . . .Highest partnership for any wicket, by Percy Holmes and
Herbert Sutcliffe for the first wicket vs. Essex in 1932

Innings and 397 runs . . . . .Largest margin of victory, vs.
Northamptonshire in 1921

341 . . . .Highest innings score, by G.H. Hirst vs. Leicestershire in 1905

318 . . . . .Highest innings score against, by W.G. Grace for
Gloucestershire in 1876

Innings and 272 runs . . .Largest margin of defeat, vs. Surrey in 1898

240 . . . . .Most wickets in a season, by Wilfred Rhodes in 1900

165 . . . . . .Fewest runs in a single match, vs. Nottinghamshire in 1888

112 . . . . .Most centuries for Yorkshire, by Herbert Sutcliffe
107 . . . . .Most wicket-keeping victims in a season, by James Binks
in 1960
23 . . . . .Lowest team score, vs. Hampshire in 1965
17 for 91 . . . . . .Best bowling figures in a match against Yorkshire, by
Harry Dean for Lancashire in 1913
17 for 91 . . . . .Best bowling figures in a match, by Hedley Verity
vs. Essex in 1933
13 . . . . .Lowest opposition score, by Nottinghamshire in 1901
10 for 10 . . . . . . .Best bowling figures in an innings, by Hedley Verity
vs. Nottinghamshire in 1932
11 . . . . . . .Most wicket-keeping victims in a match, by David Bairstow
vs. Derbyshire in 1982
7 . . . . . .Most wicket-keeping victims in an innings, by David Bairstow
vs. Derbyshire in 1982

THE SEVEN OLD AND NEW WONDERS OF YORKSHIRE

In 2005 the BBC ran a series to choose the seven wonders of each of eight regions of England. Though it was paired with Lincolnshire for the purposes of the series, Yorkshire provided most of the choices for the programme. They were:

Flamborough Head. A long chalk headland between Filey and Bridlington on the North Sea coastline.

Hornsea Mere. Yorkshire's largest freshwater lake a mile (1.6 km) from the North Sea at Hornsea.

Malham Cove. A limestone cliff and pavement near Malham in north Yorkshire.

Spurn Head. A 3 mile (4.8 km) tip of Yorkshire's coast around the mouth of the Humber.

Thorne and Hatfield Moors. The largest peat bogs in Britain, northeast of Doncaster.

The Three Peaks. Whernside, Ingleborough and Pen-y-Ghent, in the Yorkshire Dales.

The Wash. England's biggest bay – an estuary separating Lincolnshire and Norfolk on the east coast.

Rather confusingly, Yorkshire also provided two of the choices for the 'north' region in the series: Aysgarth Falls in the Dales and the River Tees, which runs along the Yorkshire–Durham border. A subsequent series then invited public votes for seven manmade wonders, this time allocating Yorkshire its own programme – though three of the picks were actually outsiders. The seven choices were:

Chatsworth. A magnificent 16th-century stately home and gardens. Actually in Derbyshire, but Yorkshire obviously considers it one of its own.

Fountains Abbey. The country's largest ruined monastery dating from 1132, near Ripon.

Lincoln Cathedral. Magnificent medieval cathedral, at one time the highest building in the world. Another selection 'borrowed' from another county.

Ribbleshead Viaduct. Stunning feat of Victorian engineering, carrying the Settle to Carlisle railway through the Yorkshire Dales.

Royal Dock Tower. Striking tower on Grimsby's docks, built in 1852 to help marshal boats into the harbour.

Salt's Mill. Huge wool mill built by Titus Salt in the 1850s as part of his Saltaire model village near Bradford, and at the time the biggest factory in Europe.

Thornborough Henge. Mile-long site of religious ritual dating back some 6,000 years.

FAMOUS YORKSHIRE FOLK – TED HUGHES

Although he spent a good deal of his life in Devon, Ted Hughes's vivid and forceful poetry is firmly rooted in the wild landscapes of his home county of Yorkshire.

Hughes was born in Mytholmroyd in west Yorkshire in 1930 – there is a plaque on his family's house on Aspinall Street – and was brought up there and in the coal-mining town of Mexborough. After winning a scholarship to Cambridge University, he worked variously as a script reader, gardener and in a zoo before his first poems were published in 1954. His first book, *The Hawk in the Rain*, was released a few years later to critical acclaim, and over the next 40 years Hughes won just about every literary award available, as well as the Queen's Order of Merit. His poems often focused on the bleak and savage but beautiful worlds of nature and animals, and his most famous work includes *Crow*, a collection of creation stories that delves into the human psyche. He wrote prose and plays as well as poetry and was an outstanding children's writer. His book *The Iron Man* was turned into a successful film and helped to bring him to a wider audience.

By the time he had established himself as a writer, Hughes was married to the American poet Sylvia Plath, who, after their separation, committed suicide in 1963. Their relationship has been the subject of much scrutiny, especially by Plath's admirers. Hughes himself remained largely silent on the matter, but spent several years editing, publishing and championing Plath's work, and he addressed the relationship in his last collection of poems, the bestselling *Birthday Letters*. Another of Hughes's partners, Assia Wevill, killed herself and their daughter Shura in similar fashion to Plath in 1969.

Hughes was poet laureate from the death of John Betjeman in 1984 until his own death in 1998, though it was thought that he was second choice for the job after another man with Yorkshire connections, Philip Larkin, turned down the post. Hughes's reputation has continued to grow since his death, and he is now counted among the greatest English poets of the 20th century.

GOD'S OWN COUNTY

Yorkshire natives like to call their home 'God's own county', but the slogan is not original to the area. The first use of the phrase 'God's own country' is claimed by New Zealand, and there is evidence of it being used as far back as the late 1800s. It has also been adopted as a tourist marketing slogan by other places, including Australia and Kerala in southern India. At some point it was tweaked slightly for use in Yorkshire - but by whom and when is unclear.

MARKS, SPENCER AND YORKSHIRE

Marks & Spencer now has some 500 shops on high streets up and down the country, but its origins are all in Yorkshire.

The business was founded by Michael Marks, a Polish-Lithuanian refugee who started out by buying a few pounds worth of fabrics and household goods from a Leeds wholesaler that he then peddled around the nearby villages from a handcart. By 1884 he had made enough money to set up his first stall on Kirkgate Market in Leeds - a Penny

Bazaar that, to excuse his poor English as well as to make things simple for his shoppers, carried the sign 'Don't ask the price, it's a penny'. A plaque now marks the site.

Marks opened other bazaars in Castleford, Wakefield and other towns, but needed extra capital to grow the business further. In 1894 he joined forces with Tom Spencer, a Skipton-born cashier at the wholesaler with which he had started out. They made a great team, Marks an ambitious salesman and Spencer a steady voice of caution who looked after the office and warehouse and, in the great Yorkshire tradition, kept a close eye on spending. Together they quickly grew the number of bazaars and shops into cities across the UK, and though both died relatively young in the early 1900s, the business continued to be a family concern under Marks's son. Spencer's initial investment for a half-share in the company was £300; Marks & Spencer now turns over some £8 billion a year.

YORKSHIRE ON TV

Yorkshire has provided a rich seam for TV producers over the years. Long-running series like *Last of the Summer Wine*, *Heartbeat* and *Emmerdale* are firmly rooted in the county, but plenty of other dramas and sitcoms have been at least partly shot here. These are twenty of the best known.

All Creatures Great and Small (1978 to 1990). Used various locations across Wensleydale, Swaledale and Arkengarthdale.

At Home with the Braithwaites (2000 to 2003). Set and filmed in Leeds.

Brideshead Revisited (1981). Nearly half of the classic TV series was shot in and around Castle Howard near Malton.

Casanova (2002). Also filmed at Castle Howard.

The Chase (2006 onwards). Set in Yorkshire and filmed in Leeds and Otley.

Emmerdale (1972 onwards). Filmed in the villages of Arncliffe and Esholt for many years, but now uses a purpose-built set on the Harewood estate near Leeds.

Heartbeat (1992 onwards). Based around the village of Goathland in the Esk Valley, where much of the filming is done. Various locations around the North York Moors also feature.

In Loving Memory (1979 to 1986). Undertakers' sitcom set in Lancashire but filmed over the border in Luddenden.

Jimmy's (1987 to 1994). Documentary hospital series, filmed at St James's University Hospital in Leeds.

Juliet Bravo (1980 to 1985). Set in Lancashire but filmed in Todmorden and elsewhere in west Yorkshire.

Last of the Summer Wine (1973 onwards). Filmed in and around Holmfirth.

The League of Gentlemen (1994 to 2002). Some scenes – including those in and around 'the local shop for local people' – were shot on the moors near Holmfirth and Marsden.

The Life and Adventures of Nicholas Nickleby (2001). Partly filmed in Grassington.

North and South (2004). Dalton Mill at Keighley was used for some exterior mill scenes.

Open All Hours (1976 to 1985). Arkwright's famous corner shop was borrowed from a store on Lister Avenue in Balby, Doncaster.

Oranges are Not the Only Fruit (1990). Partly shot in Todmorden.

Sparkhouse (2002). Shot in Hebden Bridge and Todmorden.

A Touch of Frost (1992 onwards). Filmed in Leeds, and most outdoor scenes are shot around west Yorkshire.

Where the Heart Is (1996 to 2006). The fictional village of Skelthwaite is an amalgamation of Slaithwaite and Marsden. The pub is the Silent Woman in Slaithwaite.

Wives and Daughters (1999). Used Wentworth Woodhouse in south Yorkshire.

THE FOURTH EMERGENCY SERVICE

Hundreds if not thousands of people have had good cause to be grateful to Yorkshire's emergency service for walkers – its mountain rescue teams.

Teams in the wilder parts of the county are on standby 24 hours a day and 365 days a year to help walkers injured or lost on the fells or moors. In the Dales rescue teams also frequently have to recover cavers or help farmers retrieve sheep stranded on crags or stuck in deep snow. Because incidents on the fells are more likely during poor conditions, many of the call-outs are during atrocious weather or in the night.

Rescue teams serving Yorkshire include the Cave Rescue Organisation (CRO) and the Upper Wharfedale, Swaledale, Kirkby Stephen and Scarborough and Ryedale teams. The CRO has attended more than 2,000 incidents since it began in 1935, and while smaller teams might attend only 30 or so a year, that's still a major commitment for its members. As the use of mobile phones becomes more widespread – and as some walkers seem to get dafter by the year – the number of incidents is increasing, testing the patience of teams engaged in the increasing number of spurious call-outs or fruitless searches.

All rescue teams are entirely voluntary, giving their time and skills free of charge and relying on sponsorship and donations from grateful walkers to pay for their equipment, facilities and training. They come from all sorts of backgrounds but share a love of the area they cover and a detailed knowledge of the terrain. Their skills would be impossible for the normal emergency services to replace.

YORKSHIRE FOOD – YORKSHIRE PARKIN

In an area with a healthy appetite for cakes and sweet things, Yorkshire parkin is probably the best known speciality.

Somewhere between a teabread and cake, parkin is a filling staple of Yorkshire afternoon tea. Although it is eaten all year round, it has come to be particularly enjoyed on 5 November to help remember another famous product of Yorkshire, Guy Fawkes. The association is so close in some places, like Leeds, that the day is known not as Bonfire Night but as Parkin Day. The source of the name is unknown, but it was probably in honour of a cook of the same or similar name who baked a particularly good version.

Parkin has spread across the north, and in 1800 Dorothy Wordsworth notes in her Lake District journals that she cooked it for her brother William. As it became more popular so recipes began to vary, alternately producing cake-like versions in one place and biscuity ones in another. Needless to say, each recipe claims to be the best and most authentic, but most agree that oatmeal, treacle and enough ginger to warm the blood are key ingredients. In Yorkshire and elsewhere it is known as a type of traditional 'cut-and-come-again' cake that will keep moist and improve over a couple of weeks and give full value for money.

A recipe for Yorkshire parkin

120 g butter

120 g golden syrup

120 g dark treacle

120 g soft brown sugar

250 g plain flour

3 teaspoon ground ginger

2 teaspoon ground cinnamon

1 teaspoon bicarbonate of soda

250 g medium oatmeal

1 egg

pinch of salt

Melt the butter over a very low heat. Add the syrup, treacle and sugar, and stir until the sugar dissolves. Sieve the flour, ginger, cinnamon, salt and bicarbonate of soda into a bowl and mix in the oatmeal. Make a well in the centre of the mix and break an egg into it. Beat, and gradually add the syrupy mixture to the bowl until you have a soft, smooth consistency. Loosen with a little milk if necessary. Pour into a greased tin or tray to a depth of an inch or so. Bake in a preheated low oven, 150°C (300°F), Gas Mark 2, for 50-60 minutes, until firm. Cool, then cut into squares. Leave for several days to obtain the best consistency - if you can wait that long. Serve with a cup of Yorkshire tea.

ENGLAND'S LONGEST WATERFALL

The biggest single unbroken waterfall drop in England as well as Yorkshire is claimed by Hardraw Force in Wensleydale. It drops more than 100 feet (30 m) down rocky cliffs and has been celebrated by artists including J.M.W. Turner and writers like William Wordsworth. There are bigger waterfalls underground - some in the Dales drop for more than 300 feet (91 m) - but none bigger above it, and after rain Hardraw Force is a spectacular sight and a thunderous sound. It is one of the few natural sights of its kind that you have to pay to see, situated in the grounds of the Green Dragon pub at Hardraw, which charges a few pounds for access up to the falls.

THE YORKSHIRE MONOPOLY BOARD

Bowers Row in the Leeds suburb of Woodlesford has the cheapest property in Yorkshire, while York Minster is the most expensive. That's according, at least, to the Yorkshire Monopoly Board, a special edition of the classic family game.

Dozens of Yorkshire locations replace the famous original London spots like Old Kent Road and Mayfair in the edition, which caused a bit of fuss on its release among locations that were priced in the lower brackets. The board takes in several major Yorkshire cities, plus sports grounds, like Headingley and Elland Road, and the fictional television villages of Aidensfield and Emmerdale. Many of the properties were put up for auction by the game's manufacturers, which explains the inclusion of locations like Pagoda House in Harrogate, home of tea and tea rooms business Bettys and Taylors. In ascending order of value, Yorkshire's Monopoly properties are:

> Bowers Row, Woodlesford
> Wellington Street, Leeds
> Ilkley Moor
> Caphouse Colliery, Wakefield
> Wilberforce House, Hull
> Elland Road, Leeds
> Valley Parade, Bradford
> Headingley, Leeds
> The Hedrow, Leeds
> Pagoda House, Harrogate
> Sunbridge Road, Bradford
> Castleford
> High Street, Northallerton
> Marfleet, Hull
> Aidensfield
> Emmerdale
> Coppergate, York
> Tadcaster Road, York
> York Street, Sheffield
> Piccadilly, Bradford
> Castle Howard
> York Minster

Stations on the board are Halifax, Humber Bridge, Leeds Bradford Airport and Doncaster, while the utilities spaces are represented by Yorkshire Electricity, Yorkshire Water and Yorkshire Bank.

YORKSHIRE'S LIGHTHOUSES

Yorkshire has 12 surviving lighthouses along its North Sea coast, put up to help protect ships in the heydays of sea trade. Though some are now automated, all but four are still operational. With the years the lighthouses were first established and, where relevant, the years they were decommissioned, Yorkshire's dozen lighthouses are:

Bridlington – 1852
Flamborough – 1806
Flamborough Chalk Tower – 1674; built as a tower and never lit
Killingholme – High, North and South Low Lights – 1831
Paull – 1836; decommissioned in 1870
Scarborough – 1806
South Gare at the mouth of the River Tees – 1884
Spurn Point – 1674; decommissioned in 1985
Thorngumbald – 1870
Whitby Harbour – 1831
Whitby High – 1858
Withernsea – 1894; decommissioned in 1972

YORKSHIRE'S UNUSUAL WORLD RECORD HOLDERS

Alongside its sporting, cultural and scientific high achievers, Yorkshire has its fair share of record holders in slightly less distinguished disciplines. Here are a dozen of the oddest world records notched up over the last few years. (Though they have all been certified as such by Guinness, not all of these achievements feature in the *Guinness Book of Records*, and some may since have been broken by equally daft people in other counties.)

Longest bouncy castle session. By the Newman Trust Charity at Priory Woods School in Middlesbrough in July 2006. The session lasted 19 hours 45 minutes.

Largest candy mosaic. By Calderdale's Looked After Children Education Service in Halifax, constructed over two days in February 2006. It measured 399.6 sq ft (37.126 sq m).

Fastest motorcycle wheelie. By Dave Rogers at Elvington Airfield near York in September 2005. He was timed at 251.86 kph (156.51 mph) over 1 km.

Oldest recipient of a porcine (pig) aortic value replacement. As if there's much competition for this, one of the oddest records in the *Guinness Book of Records*. The holder is Harry Driver of Wetherby, who was aged 76 years and 214 days when he underwent the surgery.

Most clothes pegs on face. By Gary Turner of York, who clipped 153 pegs onto his face in September 2002.

Largest air guitar ensemble. Recorded at the Hillsborough ground of Sheffield Wednesday FC in January 2007 by a crowd of 29,000 people. Levels of involvement varied considerably according to different reports.

Most lifts of the back end of a car. Achieved by Mark Anglesey of Rotherham in 2003. He lifted up the back end of a Mini Metro to a height of 12 to 18 inches (30-45 cm) off the ground 580 times in an hour.

Fastest underwater bog snorkel. By Joanne Pitchforth of Heckmondwike, who covered a 120 yard (110 m) course in one minute 35 seconds in August 2007.

Oldest living woman. Florrie Baldwin, born in Hunslet in 1896 and now living in a nursing home in Pudsey, is Britain's oldest living woman. She attributes her longevity to eating a fried egg sandwich every day.

Oldest ever goldfish. 'Tish', owned by Hilda Hand of Thirsk, was won at a funfair in Doncaster in 1956 and lived until 1999.

The world's largest maize maze. Claimed by York Maze, which covers an area equivalent to 15 football pitches. Opens to the public from late July to September each year.

Most pantomime dames gathered in one place. A total of 32, organised by the Theatre Royal in York in December 2007. Like many of these records, it was claimed by virtue of no one else having attempted it.

YORKSHIRE SAYINGS

'Yorkshire born and Yorkshire bred, strong in the arm and weak in the head.'

THE MENU FROM THE FEAST OF CAWOOD

After being chosen as the next Archbishop of York in the mid-15th century, George Nevill decided to throw a bit of a party. As was the way at the time, the event had to be bigger and better than those that came before it, so Nevill and his brother the Earl of Warwick decided to push the boat out. The feast in January 1466 at Cawood Castle, between York and Selby, lasted several days and is thought to be the most gargantuan in English history. Records from the time noted what had been prepared, and show that Nevill's 2,500 guests worked their way through:

25,000 gallons of wine • 5,500 hot and cold venison pasties •
5,000 hot and cold custards • 4,000 baked tarts • 4,000 mallards
and teals • 4,000 pigeons • 4,000 rabbits • 2,000 chickens •
2,000 geese • 1,200 quails • 1,000 capons • 1,000 muttons •
600 pikes and breams • 500 stags, bucks and does • 500 partridges •
400 plovers • 400 swans • 400 woodcocks • 300 jellies •
300 pigs • 300 veals • 300 tuns of ale • 300 cranes • 200 kids
(goats, not children) • 200 pheasants • 100 oxen • 100 peacocks •
100 curlews • 12 porpoises and seals • 6 wild bulls •
1 pipe of ypocras (spiced wine)

The feast required 1,000 cooks, 500 kitcheners and 500 scullions to prepare it, and 1,000 servants to serve it. And presumably a few people to do the washing up, too. Not that it all did Nevill much good in winning favour with important people; a few years after the feast he fell out with King Edward IV, had his estate confiscated and was thrown into prison.

DOES IT ALWAYS RAIN IN YORKSHIRE?

No, it doesn't. It's a common complaint from visitors to Yorkshire that it always seems to be wet, but residents of the county know better. Yorkshire is actually one of the drier areas of Britain, receiving only just over half as much rain as Scotland and a third less than the northwest. Its county-wide average is about 32.6 inches (828 mm) of rain a year, just below England's average of 33 inches (840 mm) and well under the UK average of 44.2 inches (1,123 mm). Only four areas of the UK, all in the south, have lower averages.

These figures are based on the 12 old regions of the now defunct National Rivers Authority, and show the average annual rainfall between 1991 and 2005.

Region	Average annual rainfall	
	inches	mm
Scotland	59.7	1,516
Wales	53.7	1,363
Southwest	48.4	1,229
Northwest	47.2	1,200
Northern Ireland	44.8	1,136
Wessex	35.2	893
Northumbrian	34.4	874
Yorkshire	**32.6**	**828**
Southern	32	812
Severn-Trent	30.7	778
Thames	28	712
Anglian	24.5	622

THE YORK MYSTERY PLAYS

York is not the only city with surviving Mystery Play cycles – Chester, Coventry and Wakefield are among those with versions of their own – but it is here that their tradition is longest, strongest and most proudly preserved.

The Plays illustrate the whole story of the Christian tradition from the Creation to the Last Judgement, each dramatising one of dozens of biblical scenes. They were first performed as part of the celebrations around the feast day of Corpus Christi each May or June as a very public display of piety, although the plays were from the start as much about theatre and entertainment as they were about religion. They would be performed on wagons, each carrying the cast for its particular story through the streets of York to a dozen or so 'playing stations'. Spectators could settle in for the day and watch each of the performances as they came around to their venue.

Despite their title, there's nothing mysterious about the plays. When they were first performed in medieval times, 'mystery' meant both a religious truth and a handicraft or trade, and the organising guilds of many of the professions of the time assumed responsibility for funding and performing each of the 48 pageants. Trades would often be allocated appropriate plays – shipbuilders, for instance, took on the dramatisation of the building of the Ark, goldsmiths the story of the

Three Kings and bakers the Last Supper. Despite their simple messages, the plays would often be lavish productions, full of references to life at the time and mixing dramatic spectacles with a good deal of playful humour. Trades would try to outdo each other for the best play, and the ordinary working men who performed the parts took their roles seriously. They were popular among York residents, but the city's church authorities were not always impressed, looking on from the Minster with unease at the raucous scenes and loose interpretation of the Bible.

There is evidence of the Mystery Plays being performed on wagons as far back as 1376, and the only surviving manuscript dates from about a hundred years later. The tradition continued until 1569, when they were ended by the clampdown on Catholic traditions. The plays were largely neglected until the early 1950s, when a large-scale production was staged at St Mary's Abbey as part of the Festival of Britain. Since then they have usually been performed in one continuous cycle at various venues, including – for the first time after those years of disapproval – the Minster, and featuring local amateurs alongside some famous acting names as part of the York Festival. More recently they have become a travelling spectacle again, using wagons and the original guilds of York in performances put on every few years. Just as they were in the Middle Ages, organisers hope the plays can become a fun and popular event for the whole community.

THE COUNTRYSIDE CODE

There are five main points of the Countryside Code, which was drawn up by the Countryside Agency – now Natural England – to help members of the public respect, protect and enjoy their natural surroundings.

Be safe – plan ahead and follow any signs

Leave gates and property as you find them

Protect plants and animals and take your litter home

Keep dogs under close control

Consider other people

THE NORTH YORK MOORS IN NUMBERS

Some facts and figures about the North York Moors National Park.

260,750 . . . . .average house price in pounds in 2007
25,500 . . . . .population living within the boundaries
10,086 . . . . .household spaces
3,093 . . . . .listed buildings
2,670 . . . . .miles (4,297 km) of watercourses
1952 .year the National Park was established
1,489 . . . . .highest point in feet (454 m) – Urra Moor
1,394 . . . . .miles (2,243 km) of public footpaths and bridleways
846 . . . . .scheduled ancient monuments
554 . . . . .area in square miles (1,434 sq km) of the National Park
235 . . . . .square miles (609 sq km) of agricultural land
189 . . . . .square miles (490 sq km) of open country
112 . . . . .parishes
108 . . . . .square miles (280 sq km) of woodland
46 . . . . .residents per square mile (2.6 sq km)
42 . . . . .conservation areas
26 . . . . .miles (42 km) of coastline
4 . . . . .square miles (10 sq km) of urban area
0.4 . . . . .square miles (1 sq km) of inland water

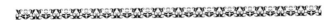

THE LOST VILLAGES

Yorkshire's records over the centuries show countless villages and towns now long gone. Many of them have been lost to erosion on the finger of coast around the Humber Estuary that tapers down to the Spurn Point peninsula. Most were small villages, though others, like Ravenser, were important trading communities, large enough to have their own MPs. A good number were lost during the 14th and 15th centuries, often the victims of great storms and floods, though there is more evidence of abandonments in 19th-century records. Settlements lost to the sea, roughly in the order in which they vanished, include:

Sand le Mere • Northrop • Hoton • Frismersk • Orwithfleet •
Penysthorp • Ravenser Odd • Saltaugh • Sunthorp • Turmarr •
East Somerte • Tharlesthorpe • Old Withernsea • Ravenser •
Newsham • Monkwike • Dimlington • Old Kilnsea • Old Newton •
Waxholme • Owthorne

A community group called Hidden Holderness now researches the lost villages and has produced a leaflet suggesting a trail around the coastline. The land here continues to shift, bringing more settlements along the coast closer and closer to the sea as the years go by.

As well as settlements lost to the waves, Yorkshire has its fair share of inland deserted medieval villages (DMVs). The highlight – and thought to be the best preserved of the 3,000 or so DMVs anywhere in England – is Wherram Percy in the Yorkshire Wolds, once a thriving farming community with several dozen houses and gardens. Many such villages were laid to waste by the Black Death in the 1340s, but Wherram Percy is thought to have survived until a few centuries later, when changes in farming made life impossible for residents. The shell of the church is the most striking part of the ghost village, but heavy excavation has uncovered plenty more evidence of life here, and the layout of other parts can also be seen in the fields. Looking down on it from the surrounding hills gives a better impression of the scale of the village that once stood here. The site is now looked after by English Heritage and has free, open access.

A MAP GLOSSARY

The Ordnance Survey maps to Yorkshire are filled with strange and wonderful words that can leave a newcomer baffled. Here are some of the more common words and their meanings.

Barrow – small hill
Beck – mountain stream
Bield – shelter, usually for sheep but sometimes for humans
Buttress – projecting part of a hill or mountain, usually a rock face
Cairn – a pile of stones marking the top of a hill or the way up to it
Col – a flat, lower area, usually between two peaks
Combe or **coomb** – a hollow on the side of a hill
Cove – a sheltered recess in a hill
Crag – steep or rugged rock
Dale – valley, from the Old Norse word *dalr*, meaning deep or low place
Dike or **dyke** – can mean either a watercourse or a bank or wall built to prevent flooding
Fell – hill, from the Old Norse word *fjall*, meaning mountain
Force – waterfall
Gill or **ghyll** – small ravine or a stream that flows down it
Gully – wide, steep cleft in a cliff

Knoll - small hill or mound
Knott - craggy, rocky hill
Laithe - farm building
Moss - flat, marshy area
Pass - passage between mountains or valleys
Ridge or **rigg** - long, narrow strip with steep drops on either side
Scar - bare, rocky outcrop
Sike or **syke** - small stream, often dry in summer
Slack - hollow area between two higher points
Snicket - alleyway
Tarn - small mountain lake
Tumulus - ancient burial area
Wash - sandbank exposed at low tide

SOME PLACE-NAMES AND THEIR MEANINGS

Sixty Yorkshire places, large and small, and how they got their names.

Allerton - either the alder tree settlement, or the farm of Aelfere or a similar Anglo-Saxon name
Ampleforth - from the place where *ampre* (sorrel) grew
Appletreewick - the farm by the apple tree
Askrigg - the ridge where ash trees grow
Aysgarth - the space or enclosure in the oak trees
Bainbridge - the bridge over the River Bain
Barnsley - the wood clearing belonging to Beorn or a similar Old English name
Batley - the wood clearing belonging to Bata or a similar Old English name
Beverley - the beaver's clearing, probably an Old English version of an earlier name
Bradford - derived from broad ford
Bridlington - the farm of Beohrtel or some similar Anglo-Saxon name
Catterick - from the Latin *cataracta* (waterfall), possibly from the nearby River Swale
Clapham - the settlement by the noisy stream
Conisbrough - the king's fortification
Dewsbury - the fortification by the stream
Doncaster - the Roman fort on the River Don
Drax - possibly derived from the Old English *drag-net*, meaning fishery
Driffield - dry field
Easby - the farm or settlement of Ese or a similar Viking name

Easingwold – the forest of Easa and his people

Filey – from 'five leys' or five forest clearings

Giggleswick – the farm of Gigle, Gikel or a similar Viking name

Goole – ditch

Halifax – possibly derived from *hali flex*, meaning holy flax field, though other theories have been suggested

Harrogate – from *Harlow gata*, meaning grey hill road

Hawes – from *hause*, meaning a narrow strip of land passing through the mountains

Haworth – hedge enclosure

Helmsley – Helm's wood or clearing

Hornsea – from the lake of the same name, meaning the water with horn-like corners

Huddersfield – the field belonging to Huder or a similar name

Hutton Magna – Hutton is a common name in Yorkshire and is derived from the Anglo-Saxon for a farm on a hill; Hutton Magna means great hutton

Ilkley – the clearing belonging to Illica or a similar name

Keighley – the clearing belonging to Cyhha or a similar name

Kettlewell – the bubbling spring or stream

Kingston-upon-Hull – the king's farm on the River Hull

Kirkbymoorside – Kirkby is a common name in Yorkshire and means the village with a kirk or church; so Kirkbymoorside means the church settlement by the head of the moor

Leeds – probably derived from the name for the tribe of people by the River Lat, now the Aire

Leyburn – the stream in the wood clearing

Masham – Maessa's ham or homestead

Middlesbrough – possibly derived from its location halfway between Durham and Whitby, or in the middle of the two

Osbaldwick – the farm belonging to Osbald

Pickering – the people of Picer, possibly an old Anglo-Saxon name

Pontefract – derived from both Latin and French meaning broken bridge

Richmond – from the old French meaning strong hill

Ripon – takes its name from the tribe that once lived there, probably called the Hrype or similar

Rotherham – settlement by the River Rother

Scarborough – the fortification of Skarth, Skarthi or a similar Viking name

Sedbergh – the flat-topped hill

Selby – settlement or farm by the willow tree

Settle – dwelling

Sheffield – Old English, from the clearing by the River Sheaf

Skipton – sheep farm

Sowerby - the muddy farm or settlement
Tadcaster - Tada's land on the site of a Roman settlement
Thirsk - from the Old Norse *thraesk*, meaning fen or lake
Thornton le Dale - Thornton is a common name meaning farm with thorn bushes
Wakefield - the field belonging to Wacca or a similar name
Wetherby - farm where wethers (castrated rams) were kept
Whitby - from the Old Norse Whiteby or white settlement, perhaps from the colour of the houses
York - derived from Eboracum, which was, in turn, possibly taken from a personal name

THE YORKSHIRE GEMSTONE

Whitby jet is Yorkshire's own gemstone, used for several thousand years in jewellery and decorative items.

Jet is formed from the fossilised remains of a particular tree from the Jurassic period about 150 million years ago, heavily compressed among sedimentary layers. Yorkshire's jet is found in a 7 mile (11 km) stretch of coastline around Whitby, and the very localised supply and difficulties of extracting it added to its value and appeal over the years.

Admired for its high polish, rich black colour and supposed medicinal or talismanic qualities, jet was popular among the Romans and Vikings in particular. But its popularity reached a peak in the second half of the 19th century, having got a useful burst of publicity from being favoured by Queen Victoria as part of her mourning dress. The jet industry was by now employing some 1,500 men, women and children in finding, extracting and fashioning it, and Whitby had several dozen workshops turning out items for export around the world. Mining jet was a hugely dangerous job, and an easier though less reliable way of obtaining it was to wait for natural erosion to expose or release new seams from the cliffs. 'Jetties' combing the coastline for fresh stocks of jet can still be seen today.

Whitby's jet industry declined in the face of cheaper but inferior jet imports and a fall in popularity. Perhaps because of its associations with mourning, jet is now considered rather sombre and has become much less widely used - though interestingly the expression 'jet black' or 'black as jet' has endured much better. A few craftsmen maintain the tradition in the town, and the Whitby Jet Heritage Centre on Church Street turns out handmade jewellery. Both the centre and the Whitby Museum have items from jet workshops of the past.

FAMOUS YORKSHIRE FOLK – FRED TRUEMAN

Though Geoff Boycott might have something to say about it, Fred Trueman is probably Yorkshire's most famous cricketing son, and in many ways its archetypal sportsman. Dour and hardworking but frequently outspoken and explosive, he is still regarded as one of England's finest ever fast bowlers, even if he is no longer around to remind everyone just how good he was in his pomp.

Although he was born on the southernmost fringes of the county in Stainton, Trueman was Yorkshire through and through. He played his first game for the county in 1949 aged 18 and, after National Service, made his England début in 1952, having an instant impact by reducing India to 0 for 4. Until his retirement in 1968 – save for a misguided return for one season four years later – he bowled his heart out for Yorkshire and England, combining a classical action, accuracy and stamina with searing pace. Although he was relatively short for a fast bowler at 5 feet 10 inches (1.78 m), his flinty competitiveness and intimidating aggression meant many opponents were beaten by him even before they arrived at the crease. In 1964 he became the first man to reach 300 Test wickets, and his final tally of 307 was an England record for many years. He took a wicket every 49 balls for his country – an outstanding average by any standards.

Trueman's fiery streak did not always go down well with umpires or the cricket authorities at Yorkshire and England, and he was forced to sit out many international matches following one clash or another. He complained of being misunderstood and shoddily treated by selectors and management, but his attitude made him a firm favourite with cricket supporters – especially in Yorkshire, where he was always revered as one of the great characters of the game rather than one of its troublemakers. He transferred his forthright style to the commentary box after retirement, and became well known for his despair at the travails of the England team in the 1980s and 1990s. He died in 2006 aged 75.

In all first-class cricket, Trueman took a staggering 2,304 wickets in 603 matches, bowling not far short of 100,000 deliveries in all. As he himself frequently reminded people, it is impossible to imagine any 21st-century cricketer bowling so much.

YORKSHIRE ACTORS

Thirty of Yorkshire's most famous stars of stage and screen, with their birthplaces.

Julian Barratt (b.1968) – Leeds
Sean Bean (b.1959) – Sheffield
Rodney Bewes (b.1937) – Bingley
Brian Blessed (b.1937) – Mexborough
Tony Capstick (1944–2003) – Mexborough
Ian Carmichael (b.1920) – Hull
Tom Courtenay (b.1937) – Hull
Judi Dench (b.1934) – York
Michael Denison (1915–98) – Doncaster
Adrian Edmondson (b.1957) – Bradford
Peter Firth (b.1953) – Bradford
Brian Glover (1934–97) – Sheffield
Richard Griffiths (b.1947) – Thornaby-on-Tees
Frankie Howerd (1917–92) – York
Gordon Kaye (b.1941) – Huddersfield
Ben Kingsley (b.1943) – Scarborough
Charles Laughton (1899–1962) – Scarborough
Maureen Lipman (b.1946) – Hull
Malcolm McDowell (b.1943) – Leeds
James Mason (1909–84) – Huddersfield
Gertie Millar (1879–1952) – Bradford
Peter O'Toole (b.1932) – Leeds
Michael Palin (b.1943) – Sheffield
Diana Rigg (b.1938) – Doncaster
Brian Rix (b.1924) – Cottingham
Patrick Stewart (b.1940) – Mirfield
Mollie Sugden (b.1922) – Keighley
Timothy West (b.1934) – Bradford
Tom Wilkinson (b.1948) – Leeds
Penelope Wilton (b.1946) – Scarborough

SMUGGLING ON THE YORKSHIRE COAST

With more than a hundred miles of rugged coastline, much of it quiet and unwatched, Yorkshire has been an ideal centre for smuggling over the centuries.

The 'free trade' of smugglers began in England on a fairly small scale as a way of dodging heavy taxation but grew over the 18th and early 19th centuries into a vast contraband industry. The short distances across the Channel to the continent meant it was more widespread and organised in the southeast, but Yorkshire had a fair number of entrepreneurial smugglers too. It may have started here as more of an export business, snatching sheep and wool from the county to ship over to Holland and beyond, but rather than return empty-handed, smugglers began to pile their ships with tea, alcohol and tobacco to send back to Yorkshire. As the ships slipped in to remote beaches, goods would be hauled up the coastline to be stored in caves or piled on to carts or caravans waiting to take them inland. Thousands of gallons of spirits could come ashore at a time, and at the peak of the trade around 80 per cent of all tea drunk in England was thought to be contraband.

Yorkshire's smuggling capital was Hull, a busy port where consignments of illegal goods could be brought in unnoticed and either sold direct to the town's large population or dispatched elsewhere along the river network. Isolated coastal places like Whitby, Staithes, Saltburn and Robin Hood's Bay were also perfect for smuggling, and at one time here practically everyone was either involved in the smuggling or supportive of it. The tight streets of villages like Robin Hood's Bay, with networks of interlinked cellars, tunnels and secret doors, meant goods could be passed invisibly around the village, and the close-knit communities made it difficult for customs people to track down smugglers. Nevertheless, there were occasional violent confrontations between revenue officials, smugglers and informants that rather belie the popular romantic image of smuggling.

One of the best places to find out more about smuggling in Yorkshire is the Smugglers Heritage Centre at Saltburn, open from Easter to September. It tells in particular the story of John Andrew, so-called King of the Smugglers, who co-ordinated the local smuggling trade from the Ship Inn next door.

TEN YORKSHIRE SAINTS

Some of the many saints with Yorkshire connections through the centuries.

Saint Paulinus. Sent from Rome in the early 7th century, he became the first Archbishop of York at the original Minster and converted King Edwin to Christianity.

Saint Hilda of Whitby. Founder of a 7th-century monastery at Whitby and revered as a teacher. There is a priory and community of Saint Hilda at Whitby's Sneaton Castle.

Saint Wilfrid. A zealous and often controversial abbot of Ripon and Bishop of York, most famous for edging the Church away from Celtic customs to Roman ones at the 7th-century Synod of Whitby.

Saint John of Beverley. A leader of the Northumbrian church to whom many miracles are ascribed. Founded a monastery on the site where Beverley Minster now stands; the church was built around his tomb.

Saint Robert of Newminster. Born near Skipton in the early 12th century and became an abbot at Whitby before joining the founders of Fountains Abbey. He later founded the abbey at Newminster, further north in Northumberland.

Saint William of York. Born in York and an archbishop there in the 12th century. After his death – supposedly from poisoning – miracles were reported at his tomb. St William's College near York Minster is named after him.

Saint Leonard of Reresby. Captured in the 13th century crusades but miraculously freed and transported back to his home town of Thrybergh in south Yorkshire to interrupt his wife's remarriage. A cross marks the spot.

Saint John of Bridlington. Born in 1319 in Thwing near Bridlington, where he lived for many years at the priory and built a reputation for miraculous powers. He is the patron of women in difficult labour.

Saint John Fisher. Born in Beverley in 1469 and executed by Henry VIII in 1535 for refusing to accept him as head of the Church of England.

Saint Margaret Clitherow. Born in York in 1556 and converted to Catholicism on marriage. She was crushed to death in 1586 for giving shelter to priests in her home on the Shambles in York.

THE YORKSHIRE BRAND

Among much fine work promoting the county, the Yorkshire Tourist Board offers a set of guidelines intended to help strengthen Yorkshire's brand among visitors. Based on research among tourists, it uncovered what it considers to be the most important brand values of the area. The words it uses to describe the essence of Yorkshire are:

Natural • Friendly and welcoming • Peaceful • Breathtaking •
Unspoilt • Relaxing • Happy and fun • Proud • Wild and rugged •
Comfortable and familiar • Warm • Exciting • Enriching •
Contemporary • Invigorating

These values are further broken down into various 'destination experiences'. So the keywords for holidays marketed as rural breaks are natural, peaceful, breathtaking, unspoilt, wild and rugged, relaxing and invigorating. Yorkshire's cities are exciting, contemporary, happy and fun. The values of the county's heritage are relaxing, proud, enriching, nostalgic, welcoming, warm and comfortable. And the seaside resorts strung along Yorkshire's east coast are happy, fun, welcoming, proud, comfortable and familiar.

How much of this is marketing jargon and how much is an accurate reflection of the county is a matter of opinion. But along with other marketing activities, it does seem to have bolstered Yorkshire's tourism, since visitor numbers have steadily increased over the last decade.

THE GREAT YORKSHIRE SEASIDE HOLIDAY

Sandcastles, donkey rides, fish and chips and Punch and Judy shows – Yorkshire's coastline once offered everything for the archetypal British seaside holiday. And while there is a faded melancholy about many of the resorts now, there is evidence of a revival in their fortunes too.

Yorkshire's seaside capital, Scarborough, claims to be Britain's first spa town and its first proper coastal resort, having championed the benefits of its waters and sea air in the 17th century. It drew in the upper and middle classes, while resorts like Blackpool catered for the workers, though the expansion of the rail network from the middle of the 19th century onwards opened up the whole coast to the masses. Other resorts, like Bridlington, Filey and Whitby, grew up in parallel to Scarborough, each offering a distinctive sense of place as well as all the usual seaside attractions.

Just as rail travel opened up the seaside resorts, so air travel cut them off again. The arrival of cheap flights to the sun and the changing tastes of the public sent coastal towns in Yorkshire and elsewhere into a downward spiral from the 1960s. The decline in visitors and investment is clear in some of the decaying old grand hotels and facilities and the empty seafronts out of season.

But Yorkshire's resorts have never lost their place in either the county's affection or the national psyche, and after years of decline there is some evidence that the great British seaside holiday is enjoying a renaissance. Whether for the nostalgia value or because holidaying at home is a cheaper or greener alternative to flights abroad, resorts are reporting increased visitor numbers. Regeneration money is freshening up facilities like Scarborough's spa complex, and a better tourist infrastructure – classier hotels, better food and cleaner beaches – has overhauled the industry's image. They may be catering now more for short breaks rather than the fortnight-long holidays of the past, but Yorkshire's resorts are back in fashion.

Yorkshire's best beaches

Holders of the Blue Flag award for clean sands and water

Bridlington - north and south beach

Cleethorpes - central beach

Filey

Hornsea

Whitby - west cliff

Scarborough - north bay

Withernsea

YORKSHIRE POEMS

'The Wensleydale Lad' – ANONYMOUS

When I were at home wi' mi' father an' mother, I nivver had na fun;
They kept me goin' frae morn to neet, so I thowt frae them I'd run.
  Leeds fair were coomin on, an' I thowt I'd have a spree,
    So I put on mi Sunday cooat, an' went right merrily.

First thing I saw were t'factory, I nivver seed one afore;
There were threads an' tapes, an' tapes and silks, to see by
            moony a score.
  Owd Ned turn'd iv'ry wheel, an' iv'ry wheel a strap,
    'Begor!' says I t'maister man, Owd Ned's a rare strong chap.'

Next I went to Leeds Owd Church – I were nivver i'one i'mi days,
An' I were maistly ashamed o'misel, for I didn't knaw their ways.
  There were thirty or forty folk, i'tubs and boxes sat,
When up comes a saucy owd fellow. Says he 'Noo, lad, tak off thi hat.'

Then in there cooms a great Lord Mayor, an' over his shooders a club,
  An' he gat into a white sack-poke, an' gat into t'topmost tub.
  An' then there cooms anither chap, I thinks they called him Ned,
  An' he gat into t'bottomest tub, an' mocked all t'other chap said.

An' then I heard a shufflin' row, I couldn't mak what aboot,
An' t'chap donn'd up i' t'white sack-poke began a-shootin' oot,
Tellin' o't'rich folk's road to Heaven, an' t'poor folk's road to Hell.
Thowt I to misel, tha silly owd fooil, tha doesn't knew t'road thisel.

So they began to preach an' pray, they prayed for George oor King;
When up jumps t'chap i' t'bottomest tub. Says he 'Good folks,
let's sing.'
I thowt some sang varra weel, while others did grunt an' groan,
Ivvery man sang just what he wad, so I sang 'Darby and Joan'.

When preachin' and prayin' were over, an' folks were gangin' away,
I went to t'chap i' t'topmost tub. Says I, 'Lad, what's to pay?'
'Why nowt,' says he, 'my lad,' Begor! i were right fain
So I clicked hod o'mi gret club stick, an' went whistlin' oot again.

ROBIN HOOD OF YORKSHIRE

Endless films, books, TV series and tourist campaigns have firmly
cemented Nottingham's status as the home of Robin Hood – but was
he actually a Yorkshireman? Local historians like to think so.

The movies and storybooks have made the story of Robin Hood's
taking from the rich to give to the poor known to millions. Separating
historical elements of his legend from the myths is difficult, and most
agree that he was more likely to have been created out of an
amalgamation of folk tales rather than one real-life hero. But whether he
is fact or fiction, there is no doubt that many of the few records that do
exist put Robin Hood firmly within Yorkshire boundaries at his birth,
death and adventures in between.

From the earliest medieval manuscripts, many of the ballads that
launched Robin Hood's legend have mentions of Yorkshire places. Some
give his birthplace as Loxley, on the outskirts of Sheffield. The stories
usually have Robin Hood as a yeoman, but there are other theories
that he was actually a nobleman of the area, perhaps even Lord of the
Manor of Loxley.

Ballads locate some of Robin Hood's adventures in south Yorkshire's
Barnsdale rather than Sherwood Forest. Barnsdale is just north of
Doncaster. There are also mentions of St Mary's Abbey in York, which at
the time would have been home to many of the rich monks and other
religious men against whom Robin Hood fought. Kirklees Priory,
meanwhile, is where he is said to have been killed and been buried,
though some historians have pointed out that the faded and neglected

gravestone here cannot date back as far as the 13th century. Access to the grave is restricted, though there are occasional organised tours to it.

The Yorkshire Robin Hood Society keeps up the campaign to appropriate the legend for Yorkshire rather than Nottinghamshire. The scrap stepped up a bit in 2005 when Doncaster decided to name its airport after Robin Hood – a marketing trick, no doubt, to pull in more foreign fliers. Nottinghamshire is distinctly unimpressed with Yorkshire's attempts to move Robin Hood north, and the row even reached the House of Commons in 2004, when MPs from the two counties put forward motions claiming Robin Hood as their own. The obvious solution to the problem – that Robin Hood's adventures took him through both Yorkshire and Nottinghamshire, perhaps because the vast forests of the time spanned both – is ignored by both counties, who would prefer to have him all to themselves.

Five Robin Hoods in Yorkshire

Robin Hood's Well, near Skelbrooke. Just off the A1, the earliest place-name associated with Robin Hood, dating back to at least the 17th century.

Robin Hood, Leeds. A separate place in its own right on 19th-century maps, now part of the sprawl of Leeds.

The **Robin Hood** pub, Hatfield. Close to Barnsdale Forest and where Robin Hood and his merry men are said – by the pub, at least – to have drunk.

Robin Hood's Wood, near Fountains Abbey. Named after a fight that involved Robin Hood's men nearby.

Robin Hood's Bay. Popular, picturesque fishing village, probably named in honour of Robin Hood rather than because of any direct connection.

WHERE 16 DALES MEET

The pretty village of Thixendale in the Yorkshire Wolds gets its name from the sixteen major and minor dales that meet there. They are:

Blubberdale • Bowdale • Breckondale • Broadholmedale •
Buckdale • Courtdale • Fairydale • Fotherdale • Honeydale •
Longdale • Middledale • Millamdale • Pluckamdale •
Warrendale • Waterdale • Williedale

Although it's not far from York and Malton, the rolling hills and dales make Thixendale one of the most remote parts of Yorkshire. It was one of the last places in England to get TV reception, provided by a transmitter only in the 1990s.

RADIO'S FIRST YORKSHIRE VOICE

Regional accents are commonplace on the radio these days, but when Wilfred Pickles took to the microphone in the 1940s his broad Yorkshire tones created a real stir among radio audiences.

Pickles, born in Halifax in 1904, started out on radio as an announcer for the BBC's north region, but was called down to London to become a national newsreader for the Home Service during the Second World War. Until Pickles's arrival, readers had delivered their bulletins in clipped, received pronunciation, and his accent sparked several complaints from baffled southern listeners, his habit of signing off with 'Good neet' in particular causing several to choke on their cocoa. Proud of his Yorkshire background, Pickles made no effort to disguise his accent, and his reception revealed the extent of England's north–south divide.

Pickles's radio début was not an attempt by the BBC to diversify its output, but – bizarre as it sounds now – a move in the interests of national security. It told complainants that the Yorkshire accent would be impossible for Germans to imitate should they ever invade Britain, take over Broadcasting House and hijack the radio to speak to the nation. And, sure enough, Pickles's stint on the news finished at the end of the war, though he went on to become a major radio celebrity as the host of the touring gameshow *Have a Go*, which drew audiences of up to 20 million in its heyday. Pickles was also among the first personalities to develop catchphrases – in his case Yorkshire-inflected lines like ''Ow do, 'are yer?'

Pickles was also a serious actor, starring in stage plays and films including *Billy Liar*. He died in 1978. His home town of Halifax has a pub called the Portman and Pickles, named after him and another local actor, Eric Portman.

FOOTBALL CHAMPIONS

Clubs from Yorkshire have won the top tier of the football league – the old Division One and now the Premier League – eleven times since it was first contested in 1888. Four different Yorkshire teams have taken the title: Sheffield Wednesday four times, Huddersfield Town and Leeds United three times apiece, and Sheffield United once.

By coincidence, Yorkshire clubs also have eleven wins in England's other premier football competition, the FA Cup, since it was first run in 1872. Sheffield's two teams, United and Wednesday, have won it four and three times respectively, while Bradford City, Barnsley, Huddersfield Town and Leeds United have each won it once.

Eleven wins in each competition isn't a bad tally, but considering Yorkshire's size, population and number of clubs, football fans often feel that the county is under-represented on the roll-call of winners. And most of those wins belong to the dim and distant past. Since the Second World War Yorkshire's only winner in either competition has been Leeds United.

League champions		FA Cup winners	
1897–8	Sheffield United	1896	Sheffield Wednesday
1902–3	Sheffield Wednesday	1899	Sheffield United
1903–4	Sheffield Wednesday	1902	Sheffield United
1923–4	Huddersfield Town	1907	Sheffield Wednesday
1924–5	Huddersfield Town	1911	Bradford City
1925–6	Huddersfield Town	1912	Barnsley
1928–9	Sheffield Wednesday	1915	Sheffield United
1929–30	Sheffield Wednesday	1922	Huddersfield Town
1968–9	Leeds United	1925	Sheffield United
1973–4	Leeds United	1935	Sheffield Wednesday
1991–2	Leeds United	1972	Leeds United

A CALENDAR OF UNUSUAL YORKSHIRE CUSTOMS

Part 2 : Autumn and Winter

More of Yorkshire's weird and wonderful traditions, old and new.

Sowerby Bridge's Rushbearing
First weekend in September

An old tradition in which locals brought rushes to the church to cover the floor, amid great ceremony. The tradition faded after stone paving was introduced but has taken place every year since being revived in the 1970s.

Mischief Night
4 November

A tradition that has died out in most places but that lingers in many Yorkshire towns, sometimes known as 'Miggy Night' or 'Goosey Night'. It began as a day on which children could play tricks on their elders without fear of punishment, but has lately become more of an excuse for vandalism that keeps police on their toes.

Dewsbury's Tolling the Devil's Knell
Christmas Eve

All Saint's Church at Dewsbury rings its bell on Christmas Eve once for every Christian year – something that these days takes a fair while. The last chime is timed to ring at midnight, honouring the birth of Jesus and the subsequent defeat of the Devil.

Goathland's Plough Stot
First Saturday after 6 January

Dates from Plough Monday, a traditional celebration in agricultural communities to mark the end of Christmas and the start of another year. There are long-sword dances and a large dinner.

Slaithwaite's Moonraking Festival
Early February

A week-long celebration of the night in 1802 when Slaithwaite smugglers, retrieving their illicit alcohol from its hiding place in the canal, successfully convinced customs and excise officials that they were actually raking out the moon. Events include a lantern procession and a re-enactment of the event.

Scarborough's Skipping Festival and Ringing of the Pancake Bell
Shrove Tuesday

A bell is rung in Scarborough at 12 noon on Shrove Tuesday as a reminder to start making pancakes. It also prompts local people to go down to the shore and start skipping – a tradition that may have started as a fertility ritual to ensure a decent crop, but that might equally have been all about having a bit of fun.

Market Weighton's Kiplingcotes Derby
Third Thursday in March

The world's oldest flat horse race, first held in 1519. The course runs for 4 miles (6.4 km) through several parishes and is open to any horse and rider. The founders stipulated that if the race ever misses a year then it should stop forever, so organisers have ensured that it has continued through snowdrifts, foot and mouth restrictions and the like.

Ripon's Moot Horn Curfew and **Bainbridge's Hornblowing**
Every evening, all year round, and every evening from late September to February

A horn sounds in Ripon every evening at 9 p.m. – four times in the market place and once outside the mayor's house. It dates back more than 1,000 years to the time when the horn indicated the start of a nightly curfew to help enforce law and order. The post of Official Hornblower continues in the town. A similar custom continues at Bainbridge, though this one was started to help direct foresters and travellers down from the surrounding hills in Wensleydale back to the village. The horn is housed in the Rose and Crown pub and hotel in Bainbridge, and is sounded at 10 p.m. every night between the Feast of the Holy Rood on 27 September and the following Shrove Tuesday.

COUNTY TOWNS

Until the reorganisation of county boundaries in 1974, Yorkshire was divided into the historic North, West and East Ridings. Their county towns or administrative headquarters were:

East Riding of Yorkshire – Beverley
North Riding of Yorkshire – Northallerton
West Riding of Yorkshire – Wakefield

The market town of the historic county of Yorkshire is York.

UNUSUAL MOUNTAIN RESCUES

The incident log books maintained by Yorkshire's various mountain rescue teams make for alarming reading, full of broken bones, stranded walkers and all-night searches. Fortunately, not every call-out is serious, although each one involves the mobilisation of hardworking teams, all of them voluntary. Here are some of the more intriguing entries from the logs of the Swaledale, Upper Wharfedale and Scarborough & Ryedale rescue teams over the last few years.

17 February 2008, Askrigg
'Team along with dogs and handlers called by North Yorkshire Police to search for a missing male who had left the Crown public house

in Askrigg on Saturday night to walk home to Hawes. Stood down almost immediately when the man arrived home (obviously with some explaining to do).'

28 October 2007, Bolton Abbey
'Called by three people stuck on three stepping stones due to flood waters. Rescued by fire service. We "assisted" the fireman in the river …'

24 June 2006, Dalby Forest
'Team requested to find missing male following a concert in Dalby Forest. The gentleman was found safe and well asleep on a picnic table in the forest.'

28 May 2006, Dow Cave
'"Well built" caver too big for narrow passage and then too fatigued for alternative route.'

24 September 2005, Hawkcliffe Wood
'Helped recover a woman who dropped down a covered four feet hole having just accepted a proposal!'

19 September 2005, Boggle Hole
'Team joined coastguards in a search for a missing 27-year-old male in the Boggle Hole area. No one was found but information later provided by the police suggested the person had gone to Scotland!'

20 May 2005, Gunnerside Gill
'Two adventurous sheep became stranded on a ledge on the aptly named Ewe Leap Scar in Gunnerside Gill. The team retrieved the sheep and returned them to their grazing.'

22 February 2005, Cropton Forest
'Team asked by police to investigate a possible missing person in a remote part of Cropton Forest following reports from a local man of "strange foot prints in the snow". The team tracked the footprints and ascertained that they returned to civilisation in the Hartoft area.'

YORKSHIRE AT THE CENSUS

The last full census in 2001 broke down its data into regions of the UK. Findings for the Yorkshire and Humber region included the following.

4,964,833 . . . . .number of people
2,064,748 . . . . .number of lived-in households
28,700 . . . . .increase in population since last census in 1991

478.6 . . . .percentage increase in population since the census of 1801
94.7 . . . . .percentage who were born in the UK
93.5 . . . . .percentage who are white
73.1 . . . . .percentage who describe their religion as Christian
51.4 . . . . .percentage of population who are female
42.4 . . . . .percentage who are employed
41.3 . . . . .percentage who are married
29.8 . . .percentage with long-term illness or 'not good' general health
23.9 . . . . . . .percentage of 16- to 74-year-olds with no qualifications
20.5 . . . . .percentage aged 0 to 15
15.5 . . . . .percentage who are divorced or widowed
13.1 . . . . .percentage of households without central heating
12.6 . . . . .percentage of households with no car or van
11.8 . . . . . .percentage of 16- to 74-year-olds educated to degree level
or higher

10.6 . . . . . .percentage of households with two or more cars or vans
9.9 . . . . .percentage of England's total population living in the region
7.6 . . . . .percentage aged 75 and over
3.5 . . . . .percentage who are unemployed
3.2 . . . . .number of people per 2.5 acres (hectare)
2.4 . . . . .average number of people per household

MOTHER SHIPTON'S PROPHECIES

Depending on your levels of cynicism, Mother Shipton is either the greatest prophet of the last 500 years or one of its biggest hoaxers. Either way, she has become part of Yorkshire legend and is a one-woman tourist attraction centuries after her death.

Born in a cave in Knaresborough in the late 15th century under the more prosaic name of Ursula Southeil, Mother Shipton was said to have been welcomed into the world by cracks of thunder, and to have been hideously ugly from birth because she had been fathered by the Devil. She apparently displayed her mystic powers from an early age, using rudimentary poetry to predict both local deaths and events of national importance, and she drew awed visitors from across the country to listen to her. She died in 1561 and was buried on unconsecrated ground around York. Over the next few centuries more of her prophecies, like the Great Fire of London, came true.

If this sounds a little farfetched, that's because it is. Mother Shipton's prophecies were published in books only well after her death, and it is now widely accepted that many of her predictions had been fabricated by others to fit retrospective events. This certainly explains Mother

Shipton's uncanny accuracy, though the failure of one of her more ambitious prophecies – that the world would end in 1881 – rather undermined confidence in her. Other of her predictions are couched in terms so vague that they could be interpreted as fitting numerous future happenings.

But while belief in the story of Mother Shipton has dissipated over the centuries, she still has a popular hold on the imagination in Yorkshire and beyond. Mother Shipton's Cave at Knaresborough, open daily from April to October and at weekends in February and March, pulls in thousands of curious visitors each year. Close to the cave is the Petrifying Well, which, having drawn tourists since 1630, claims to be England's oldest visitor attraction and supposedly turns everything dropped in it to stone. This is one of the few stories around Mother Shipton that has some basis in fact, since the mineral-rich cascading waters do actually harden or 'petrify' any items placed in the well – albeit over months rather than instantaneously as the legend has it.

Ten Mother Shipton prophecies

The dissolution of the monasteries

The defeat of the Spanish Armada

The Civil War

The Great Plague

The Great Fire of London

The Industrial Revolution

Motorised transport

The telephone

Tunnels through hills

Space exploration

YORKSHIRE FOOD – FISH AND CHIPS

Yorkshire is far from the only place to count fish and chips among its most popular meals, but its close connections probably entitle it to call itself the capital of the industry.

With its North Sea coastline and long fishing heritage, Yorkshire is prime territory for what was Britain's favourite supper until it was overtaken by curry. Fish had been fried and sold in Yorkshire for some time before it was paired with chips by some imaginative shopkeeper, the identity of whom is the source of disagreement between northern and southern camps. But while there is debate over who first coined the dish, Yorkshire can certainly claim both the oldest surviving fish and chip shop in the world – in Yeadon, near Leeds – and the country's most successful ever fryer – Harry Ramsden.

Just a mile north of Yeadon in Guiseley, Ramsden opened his first shop in a wooden hut in 1928. Brisk trade allowed him to move three years later to a swisher, restaurant-style emporium next door, and his concept of sit-in fish and chips rather than newspaper-wrapped takeaways soon attracted hordes of diners. Some 80 years after that first branch opened and 50 years after its founder retired, Harry Ramsden is now a chain of hundreds of branches with franchises overseas as well as in its British heartlands. The company was first floated on the Stock Exchange then bought by a succession of food service companies, which have worked their brand hard, extending into motorway service stations and frozen products for supermarkets.

Ramsden did much to increase the popularity of fish and chips, across Britain as well as Yorkshire. Cheap, filling and instant, fish and chips were particularly popular in his lifetime among working-class communities, though it is now a remarkably classless dish, increasingly found on gastropub and restaurant menus.

But while it has spread around the world, Yorkshire fish and chip fans swear that small differences make their county's version of the dish best, and true aficionados could probably tell where in Britain they were standing by the fish and chip shop menu in front of them. While cod fried in oil is common in the south, for instance, haddock and dripping are the norm in the north. A scallop is a mollusc in the south and a slice of potato in batter in the north, while 'scraps' or 'shoddy' are tiny bits of frying leftovers probably unheard of south of the Watford Gap. It has a language all of its own, but while other food fashions come and go, Yorkshire has stayed loyal to its fish and chips.

Ten corny fish and chip shop names in Yorkshire

The Battered Friar, York
Chip-in-Dales, Otley
The Codfather, Sheffield
The Dishy Fish, Knottingley
Frydays, Scarborough
Fryer Tuck, Leyburn
The Frying Machine, Leeds
The In-plaice, Bradford
Jenny's Plaice, Wakefield
Northern Sole, Sheffield

❀❀❀❀❀❀❀❀❀❀❀❀❀❀❀❀❀❀❀❀❀❀❀❀❀❀❀❀❀❀

YORKSHIRE IN THE DOMESDAY BOOK

The Domesday Book of 1086 offers a fascinating snapshot of Yorkshire. Divided into the three Ridings, here are its tallies of place-names and people.

	Places	**Population**
West Riding	719	3,192
North Riding	639	2,014
East Riding	424	2,363
Total	**1,782**	**7,569**

Since the Domesday survey counted only heads of family, most experts think that the population must be multiplied by four or five to give a more realistic total of residents. That would put the population of Yorkshire at the time at between 30,000 and 38,000.

❀❀❀❀❀❀❀❀❀❀❀❀❀❀❀❀❀❀❀❀❀❀❀❀❀❀❀❀❀❀

THE STORY OF THE YORKSHIRE TERRIER

The Yorkshire Terrier – sometimes known, like its human counterparts, as a Yorkie – has a good claim to be one of the county's biggest exports.

Regarded by fans as an affectionate and loyal friend and by critics as an irritating, aggressive toy, it has become one of the most popular of all breeds in America as well as Britain, partly because it has somehow been adopted as the favoured pet of celebrities on both sides of the Atlantic. Its miniature size and long, fine, groomable hair makes it the ideal choice for those who prefer their dog to be a handheld accessory than a working animal. But this popular image of the Yorkshire Terrier today is a long way from its original characteristics. Selective breeding has made it one of the smallest dogs – usually now weighing around 6½ lb (3 kg) or so and measuring no more than 8 inches (20 cm) in height – but it was originally considerably bigger with much less glamorous uses.

The dog was bred from the mid-19th century by Scots, who came down to Yorkshire and Lancashire in search of work in the mills, mines or factories in increasing numbers after the Industrial Revolution. They brought with them various breeds of terriers, and although the exact bloodline is unclear, the Yorkshire version probably grew out of the crossing of these with English and, surprisingly, Maltese breeds. Like the terriers before it, the Yorkie was used as a ratting dog, small and nimble enough to seek out vermin in the mills, mines and homes.

It was also sometimes used in hunting or placed in rather unsavoury competitions where terriers would compete to kill the most rats as quickly as possible. The Yorkshire Terrier name was in wide use by the 1870s, and their popularity has grown exponentially ever since.

Famous Yorkies have included 'Huddersfield Ben', a dog that became well known after sweeping the board at ratting contests and dog shows and that is sometimes regarded as the patriarch of the breed, not least because he was in high demand as a stud dog. In 1997 the breed scooped the overall Best in Show prize at Crufts for the first time, further increasing its popularity.

Ten celebrity Yorkshire Terrier owners

Victoria Beckham, singer
Simon Cowell, TV personality
Missy Elliott, singer
Paris Hilton, socialite
Jose Mourinho, football manager
Tara Reid, actress
Joan Rivers, comedienne
Britney Spears, singer
Justin Timberlake, singer
Bruce Willis, actor

ON THE TRAIL OF LAST OF THE SUMMER WINE

For a show about people in the twilight of their lives, it is ironic that the BBC's *Last of the Summer Wine* has become the world's longest running sitcom. The show, which was launched in 1973 and now has its 30th series in its sights, has also – for good or bad – provided an introduction to Yorkshire for many millions of people in Britain and around the world.

The series is set in and around the town of Holmfirth, a few miles south of Huddersfield in the Holme Valley. It has enjoyed a substantial tourist industry on the back of its connections, and the centrepiece is The Summerwine Exhibition, a small museum with photos, films and memorabilia from the series. It incorporates Compo's house in the series, and also houses 'The Wrinkled Stocking' tearoom, named in Nora Batty's honour. The White Horse Inn at nearby Jackson Bridge has been used as a filming location ever since the series began and now keeps something of a shrine to the series.

Holmfirth receives thousands of TV tourists each year, and many of them take the 'Summer Wine' coach tour organised by the people at

Sid's Café - a working café outside of filming times. You can even stay at Nora Batty's house in the town, apparently furnished in her style. The series has brought a lot of money to Holmfirth, although the disruption from endless filming and tourism has sometimes led to tension between TV producers and residents.

PRISONER OF WAR CAMPS

A survey by English Heritage has found records of Second World War prisoner of war camps in more than 30 locations across Yorkshire. Some were previously farm buildings, holiday camps or, in three instances, racecourses, pressed into emergency service as prisoner camps during the war, while others were purpose built to hold enemy men. Most are now long gone, though some buildings survive to varying extents. Their locations in Yorkshire were:

Barlow • Bishop Burton, Beverley • Boston Spa •
Boythorpe • Catterick • Doncaster Racecourse • Easingwold •
Farnley, Leeds • Gilling • Goole • High Green, Sheffield •
Horsforth, Leeds • Knaresborough • Little Thirkleby •
Lodge Moor, Sheffield • Malton • Naburn, York •
Norton in Malton • Norton, Sheffield • Otley •
Overdale Park, Skipton • Ravensfield Park, Rotherham •
Ripon Racecourse • Rudston • Scriven, Knaresborough •
Selby • Snaith • Storwood • Tadcaster • Ure Bank, Ripon •
Welton, Brough • York Racecourse

The best place to find out more about life in the camps and elsewhere during wartime Yorkshire is at the Eden Camp Modern History Theme Museum. The camp at Malton, built in 1942 to house German and Italian prisoners, has been imaginatively converted into an interesting museum, each of the surviving huts adapted to tell different parts of the story of the war. Tel. 01653 697777 or visit www.edencamp.co.uk.

FAMOUS YORKSHIRE FOLK – JOSEPH PRIESTLEY

Though he is best remembered for his scientific achievements, Joseph Priestley was a Yorkshireman of a staggering range of talents, way ahead of his time in his political and religious beliefs as well as his science.

Priestley was born in 1733 in Birstall, southwest of Leeds. The son of a cloth maker and dresser, he was precociously talented from an early age, learning numerous languages and reading insatiably. He was educated as a preacher, picking up the dissenting, tolerant views that informed his whole life but that often made him unpopular. He also set up as a teacher, passing on the vast knowledge that led him to write more than 150 books on history, theology, politics and other subjects – sometimes because he was so fed up with the poor quality books available to his pupils.

Though it was far from his main career, Priestley always kept his hand in with science, and his first serious experiments led him to write about electricity. Although his work was acclaimed and he became a Fellow of the Royal Society, he took up teaching and preaching jobs in Warrington – where he met his wife, Mary Wilkinson – and Leeds. Somehow finding the time to continue his scientific research, he turned now to the properties of gases. Among his early achievements were to find a technique for dissolving carbon dioxide into water, thus winning for himself the dubious honour of the father of the fizzy drinks industry.

Working as a well-paid and lightly worked teacher for the Earl of Shelburne in the early 1770s gave Priestley more time for science. His experiments led him to discover a gas 'of exalted nature' that accelerated fire and that was intoxicating to breathe – oxygen. Although other scientists, including Antoine Lavoisier, can lay claim to the original discovery and to the title of the father of modern chemistry, Priestley's influence was substantial. He also isolated and identified other important gases, including sulphur dioxide, nitrogen dioxide and nitrous oxide (laughing gas), and in doing so blew away a theory of the day that there was only one true 'air'.

Priestley moved to Birmingham to take up a new preaching post in 1780 and joined the Lunar Society, an influential group of academics and scientists whose work helped to prompt the Industrial Revolution. By now he had developed very liberal views that he publicised in books and pamphlets, strongly opposing the church establishment to pave the way for Unitarianism and supporting the revolutions in France and America. As suspicion about his motives spread, he suffered attacks on his home, church and laboratory from supporters of the king and Church. He emigrated to America in 1794, and was hailed as a free-thinking friend of the new republic, making an influential friend in future President Thomas Jefferson. He died in 1804, and the house where he lived in Pennsylvania is now a museum to him.

Priestley's achievements have often been undervalued, perhaps because it is difficult to know just where to begin when assessing his work. He is remembered in Yorkshire through Warrington's Priestley College, and there are statues of him in both Birstall and Leeds.

YORKSHIRE'S BEST MUSEUMS AND GALLERIES

Mark Fisher's book *Britain's Best Museums and Galleries* lists some 350 places, of which 35 are to be found in Yorkshire and Humberside. By his system of star rating, where one is worth a detour and five is the best, there are 21 museums or galleries with either two stars (for 'the best in the region'); three (for 'collections of national importance'); or four (for 'the best national collections').

Four stars
Harewood House, Leeds
Temple Newsam, Leeds

Three stars
Cartwright Hall Art Gallery, Bradford
Castle Howard, near Malton
Ferens Art Gallery, Hull
Graves Art Gallery, Sheffield
Leeds City Art Gallery
National Media Museum, Bradford
National Railway Museum, York
Royal Armouries, Leeds
York Art Gallery
Yorkshire Sculpture Park, Wakefield

Two stars
Beck Isle Museum of Rural Life, Pickering
Beningbrough Hall, York
Henry Moore Institute and the Centre for the Study of Sculpture, Leeds
Lotherton Hall, Aberford, Leeds
Mappin Museum and Art Gallery
National Coal Mining Museum, Caphouse Colliery, Wakefield
Wakefield Art Gallery
Weston Park Museum and Art Gallery, Sheffield
Yorkshire Museum, York

THE ENGLISH SPA

Although visitors these days are more likely to come for a conference than for the water, Harrogate owes much of its development to its years as a spa town.

The medicinal qualities of Harrogate's waters were discovered in the 16th century by William Slingsby, who found that a well's water tasted much like the drinks he had experienced at a spa on the continent. His friend Timothy Wright, physician to Queen Elizabeth, christened it 'The English Spa', and others soon championed the benefits of drinking or bathing in the iron- and sulphur-rich waters. As more springs were discovered over the years, public bathing houses, hotels and treatment centres were built around them, and Harrogate grew from a small village into a sizeable spa town. It also gave rise to the infamous Harrogate Headaches, brought on by the sulphur fumes of the wells.

The arrival of the railway in the 1840s made Harrogate more accessible, and at its peak some 75,000 people a year were coming to take the waters, said to be able to cure numerous complaints, including gout and rheumatism. Royalty and wealthy patients in particular flocked to the town for recuperation, prompting a host of elegant buildings and facilities to serve them. The grandest building of all was the Royal Baths complex of Turkish baths, mud baths, steam rooms and hydrotherapy treatments staffed by a legion of doctors and masseurs, opened in 1897.

As the 20th century wore on, medical opinion moved away from regarding water as a panacea. As the NHS grew, visitor numbers fell, and many of the hydrotherapy buildings closed. But the revival of interest in luxury spa treatments has helped Harrogate. The Turkish Baths are now restored to their Edwardian grandeur, and the town continues to market itself as a spa destination – even if treatments are now a little more sophisticated than the baths in peat from the moors of the past.

Harrogate's reputation has also produced a nice sideline in mineral water over the years, and bottled spa water was a major export in the early 20th century. While the exponential growth of other mineral water brands has diminished sales, a big new bottling plant in the town is revitalising the industry.

A side effect of the emptying of some of the large old hotels and treatment centres has been to establish Harrogate as one of Britain's leading towns for conferences and exhibitions. Its history is meanwhile celebrated at the town's Royal Pump Room, where interesting exhibits from the town's spa history include the Stinking Well, a sulphurous spring with waters that are optimistically billed by the museum as 'an unforgettable experience'.

THE YORKSHIREMAN'S COAT OF ARMS

According to an old joke, the Yorkshireman's coat of arms is made up of a fly, a flea, a magpie and a flitch (cured side) of bacon. The first three creatures are supposed to represent particular characteristics: a fly because it will drink with anyone; a flea because it will bite anyone; and a magpie because it will talk endlessly with anyone – all supposedly just like Yorkshire people. Rather unpleasantly, the bacon is supposed to be no use until it is hung – just like a Yorkshireman. The source of the joke is unknown, but most Yorkshiremen suspect it started over the border in Lancashire.

TEN LITERARY LOCATIONS

Yorkshire's strong cultural heritage means there are literary locations dotted across the county. The two most famous – Haworth, home to the Brontë sisters, and Whitby, the inspiration for Bram Stoker's *Dracula* – are profiled elsewhere in this book, but here are ten more stops on a literary tour of Yorkshire.

Bootham, York. W.H. Auden, usually considered among the finest English poets of the 20th century, was born at number 54 on this street. It is marked by a blue plaque.

The Brynmor Jones Library, Hull University. The workplace of poet Philip Larkin for 30 years. He lived close by and is buried in the Cottingham cemetery. The university has a large archive of Larkin's writings.

Croft on Tees. The rectory here was a childhood home for Charles Dodgson – aka Lewis Carroll. He started writing here and may have drawn on it for aspects of *Alice in Wonderland*.

Malham Tarn, near Skipton. Peaceful lake high in the Dales that inspired Charles Kingsley's novel *Water Babies*.

Rudston. Novelist Winifred Holtby was born, lived and died, aged just 37, in this small village near Bridlington. She is buried in the village's churchyard.

Shandy Hall, Coxwold. The home for eight years of Laurence Sterne, author of *Tristram Shandy*. Restored by the Laurence Sterne Trust and now open to the public.

St Michael and All Angels Church, Hubberholme. The churchyard in Upper Wharfedale in the Yorkshire Dales where the ashes of versatile writer J.B. Priestley were scattered. There is a plaque remembering him at the church.

St Thomas' Church, Heptonstall. The churchyard has the grave of poet Sylvia Plath. Supporters resentful of her former husband Ted Hughes chiselled out Hughes from her name on the gravestone's inscription.

Whitby Abbey. Caedmon, usually considered to be the first English poet, composed much of his work here in the 7th century.

Winestead. In this small village near Hull in the Holderness area of the East Riding the metaphysical poet Andrew Marvell was born in 1621.

YORKSHIRE AND THE BIRTH OF RUGBY LEAGUE

Yorkshire is the official birthplace of ruby league, and continues to be one of the sport's most important heartlands.

The story of the game's creation is a good illustration of England's north-south divide and of the fierce determination of Yorkshire in particular. It grew out of the creeping professionalism of rugby, which for years had been a sport played for pleasure and pride and not for money. In southern counties, where rugby was largely an upper- or middle-class activity, amateurism wasn't a problem, but in Yorkshire and Lancashire, where teams were drawn from the mines, mills and factories, players were struggling to train, play and travel while simultaneously holding down demanding jobs. Some clubs began offering 'broken time' money to compensate working-class players for their loss of earnings. And as payments became more common and competition intensified, clubs offered larger sums to lure the star players away from their rivals.

Rugby's authorities – largely based in the south – were horrified at the way the game was turning professional. A succession of inquiries into payments and transfers in the early 1890s punished several clubs with suspensions, fuelling resentment across the north. In July 1895 a dozen clubs resigned from the Yorkshire rugby union in protest and were firmly rebuffed by the authorities when they made efforts to continue their association in some way. So they severed all links and, with their counterparts from Lancashire, set up a new Northern Union to administer their sport. The birth of rugby league is usually dated to 29 August 1895, when 22 clubs from Yorkshire and Lancashire got together at the George Hotel in Huddersfield to officially form the Union. The George Hotel still stands on Huddersfield's main square, and a plaque recalls the meeting.

Dozens more clubs followed in breaking away from the amateur union over the next few years. The two unions continued playing under the same rules at first, but after similar breakaways in Australia and New Zealand, the rules began to change. When the Northern Union changed its name to the Rugby Football League in 1922 the sport began to be more widely known as rugby league – and with 13 rather than 15 players a side, a different scoring system and various other changes, it became a recognisably different sport from that played by clubs in the old rugby union.

Players and supporters of rugby league and rugby union have viewed each other with suspicion if not hostility ever since the schism, and league looked on with some amusement when the old union sport finally followed it into formal professionalism nearly a century later. The heartlands of both sports in the north and south respectively have changed very little, and Yorkshire has provided many of rugby league's powerhouse clubs in the years since. In the 2008 season it had seven of the 12 clubs in the main Super League: Bradford Bulls, Castleford Tigers, Huddersfield Giants, Hull FC, Hull Kingston Rovers, Leeds Rhinos and Wakefield Wildcats.

YORKSHIRE INDUSTRY – COAL

Mining coal in Yorkshire has always been much more than a job. Full of social and political connotations, for generations it defined large swathes of the county like no other industry. No matter how dirty and dangerous the work, it is an element of Yorkshire's history of which it has been – and remains – fiercely proud.

Yorkshire's coal mining grew slowly and declined suddenly. There is evidence of small-scale mining as far back as Roman times, though until the 18th century coal was mostly retrieved from the surface. It quite literally powered the county's economy and drove Britain's Industrial Revolution, which, in turn, increased demand for fuel and sent miners deeper underground for coal. The arrival of canals and then the railways accelerated exports out of Yorkshire's coalfields, making the industry ever bigger – but not safer. Mining was tough, dangerous work, and there was an appalling catalogue of deaths from explosions and shaft accidents over the centuries.

As more pits were opened, villages grew up around them. The job of mining passed down through generations of families, and coal began to define whole communities. They were knitted closer together by the solidarity of miners and the strength of the unions, which had led ongoing conflicts with mine owners over working conditions and pay. After the industry was nationalised at the end of the Second World War miners' grievances were redirected towards the government. Tensions increased as the market declined and collieries began to merge of close, leading to the bitter miners' strike of 1984 and 1985.

What began as a protest against the pit closure programme has come to be seen as a furious class struggle between the workers of the north and Margaret Thatcher's London government. What angered the miners was that in most cases pits were closed not because the coal had run out or because demand had decreased, but because they were suddenly out of fashion. Imported coal and gas were cheaper, and other forms of power were considered more efficient.

The closures that followed the strike caused an enormous jolt that still reverberates around Yorkshire. In 1983 it had some 60 pits, but now there are just three still turning out coal – Hatfield, Kellingley and Maltby. Thousands of jobs were lost, mining villages were ripped apart, and the ripples were felt in larger places like Barnsley, Doncaster and Wakefield. Some of the towns along the old coalfields have managed to develop other sources of employment to replace coal, but the sense of discontent and betrayal is still keenly felt elsewhere.

The best place to find out more about Yorkshire's coal heritage is the National Coal Mining Museum, built from the disused Caphouse Colliery near Wakefield. A cage lift takes visitors hundreds of feet underground to see the conditions workers mined in from the late 18th century until its coal ran out in 1985.

Yorkshire pits of the past – 50 lost local collieries

Acton Hall • Allerton Bywater • Askern • Barnburgh • Bentley • Brodsworth • Brookhouse • Bullcliffe Wood • Caphouse • Cortonwood • Darfield • Dearne Valley • Denby Grange • Dinnington • Emley Moor • Ferrymoor • Frickley • Fryston • Gascoigne Wood • Glasshoughton • Goldthorpe • Grimethorpe • Hickleton • Houghton • Kilnhurst • Kinsley • Kiveton Park • Ledston Luck • Manvers • Markham • Newmarket Silkstone • North Gawber • North Selby • Nostell • Redbrook • Riccall • Rossington • Royston • Saville • Sharlston • Silverwood • South Kirby • Stillingfleet • Thurcroft • Treeton • Wath • Wheldale • Whitemoor • Wistow • Woolley

THE RISE AND FALL OF THE RAILWAY KING

A transport visionary who put York at the heart of the rail network or a fraudulent chancer who wrecked people's lives? George Hudson divides opinion among rail historians like few others.

Born in Howsham near York in 1800, Hudson initially worked in a draper's shop in York, rising to the position of partner, but a family inheritance of some £30,000 in his twenties changed the direction of his life. Hudson invested much of the money in the North Midland Railway, and soon secured permission to bring the railway to York. By 1839 a line had been built to link the city to the towns further west, and soon it was linked all the way down to London. Hudson then looked north to extend lines up to Newcastle, and by 1844 he had a network of 1,000 miles (1,610 km) of track, reaching from the southeast of England to Scotland. Securing permission for his expansions was made easier by Hudson's side-career as a politician; he was Lord Mayor of York and MP for Sunderland.

Hudson was called the 'Railway King' during the decade of 'railway mania', when speculators piled in to the railway market and share prices rocketed. At its peak, hundreds of new rail companies were being formed every year, and half of all Britain's investment was going into trains. It changed Yorkshire forever, opening up travel to ordinary people, providing work for thousands of labourers and fuelling the industrial growth of the county.

Like many stock market bubbles since, the railway mania couldn't last. Hudson was unable to make the new rail empire pay as he had promised, and suspicions about his business dealings began to mount. When share prices inevitably deflated towards the end of the 1840s, Hudson was blamed for ruining many speculators. Inquiries uncovered mis-selling, bribes and falsified accounts across his businesses, and when it became clear he couldn't pay back the money he owed, he was briefly imprisoned for debt at York Castle. Bankrupt, he then fled to the continent, still plotting new rail lines and money-making schemes. He died in 1871.

Hudson's demise was taken by many to illustrate the perils of ambition and chasing money. Feelings towards him have softened a little over the years, and he is generally now credited with linking York and Yorkshire into England's rail network. York has a George Hudson Street near its railway station, and there is a plaque to him on the site of the draper's shop on Goodramgate where he started working - though not yet a statue to him. The excellent National Railway Museum in York has lots of material about the growth of the railways in Yorkshire and elsewhere.

A GLOSSARY OF SHEEP FARMING TERMS

The lingo of Yorkshire sheep farmers can be baffling to the uninitiated.
Here are the meanings of some of their terms.

Cade – a lamb raised by hand
Cast ewe – an older ewe brought down from the hills for one last breeding
Couples – ewes and their lambs
Draft ewe – a ewe past her productive life
Ewe – a female sheep after mating
Gimmer – a young female sheep before its first shearing
Heafing – sheep's natural instinct for their 'home' ground that keeps them within their particular patches of hillside or coming back to them after being moved
Hogg or **hogget** or **hoggerel** – a young male sheep before its first shearing
Inbye – sheep's land fenced between fields and open fells
Intake – pasture fenced from the fells
Kemps – coarse hair
Lug mark – a small hole made in the ear to distinguish a sheep and identify its owner
Ram – an uncastrated male sheep of one year or older
Shearling – a young sheep after its first shearing and before its second
Smit mark – chemical dye on the fleece, identifying a sheep's owner
Teg – a sheep in its second year
Tup – the mating of a ram and ewe; also a name for ram
Wether or **wedder** – a castrated male

THE FAIRYTALE OF YORKSHIRE

Cottingley near Bradford was the scene of the world's most famous appearance of fairies – or, as it subsequently became clear, one of its biggest hoaxes.

Yorkshire's most famous fairytale began in the late 1910s when two young cousins, Elsie Wright and Frances Griffiths, claimed to have seen fairies at Cottingley and to have photographed themselves playing with them. Their evidence got the backing of Sherlock Holmes creator Sir Arthur Conan Doyle, a keen supporter of spiritualism and psychic phenomena, who claimed in a magazine article in 1920 that he could find no sign of tampering with the photos. News of the find appeared in the *Yorkshire Post* and other papers, and despite a very healthy dose of Yorkshire scepticism on the part of the *Post*'s journalist, the story spread around the world. After gathering more evidence from the girls, Conan Doyle wrote a book on the subject in 1922.

Decades of controversy followed about the authenticity of the photos, with media and the public split on whether to accept the story or not. Like Conan Doyle, many people were desperately keen to believe in fairies and otherworldliness and were prepared to take the girls on trust. Several claimed to have seen fairies elsewhere in Yorkshire. But others were more wary, pointing out the scope for camera trickery and suggesting that the fairies looked suspiciously like those drawn in children's fairytale books of the time. Nevertheless, the pictures became some of the most reproduced photographs in history, and the girls were pursued by the media all their lives. Wright emigrated to the US to escape the attention, but found interest there to be just as high and returned to the UK.

Then in the early 1980s one of the cousins finally confessed that it had all been a rather simple hoax. Having kept the secret for more than 60 years to protect the pride of Conan Doyle and others who had believed them, she explained that pictures of fairies had been cut out and propped up with hatpins. But not even that ended the controversy, since the younger cousin, aged ten at the time the story broke, claimed that at least one of the photos had been genuine and that they had indeed seen fairies at Cottingley.

The willingness of people to believe in the existence of fairies continues to propagate the myth nearly a century after the event. There have been endless books and several films about the saga, and Cottingley continues to receive curious tourists hoping for a glimpse of the fairies. Some of the photos and camera equipment are housed in the National Media Museum in Bradford, and various collections of the photos, negatives and slides have sold for thousands at auction.

THE STEEPEST ROADS

The steepest stretch of driveable road in Yorkshire is between Rosedale Abbey and Hutton-le-Hole in the North York Moors. Called Chimney Bank, it rises at a gradient of 1 in 3, with a number of hairpin bends thrown in for good measure. Coaches and caravans are warned against tackling it, and cyclists are advised to dismount before going down it, though many seem to like the challenge of climbing up. Though there are other 1 in 3s in the country, Chimney Bank usually vies with the Hardknott Pass in the Lake District for the title of the steepest road in England.

Other steep stretches in Yorkshire include Staithes Hill and Sutton Bank near Helmsley, with gradients of 1 in 3.5 and 1 in 3.8 respectively. The nicely named Park Rash near Kettlewell in the Dales rates 1 in 4, while Wass Bank near Byland Abbey and Greenhow between Pateley Bridge and Grassington are both nearer 1 in 4.5. The highest road in Yorkshire is over Fleet Moss from Buckden to Hawes, which reaches 1,934 feet (589 m).

THE YORKSHIRE REGIMENT

Of all the regiments in the British army, the Yorkshire Regiment is the only one to be named for a county. It was formed in its current shape in 2006 on the amalgamation of three historic infantry regiments – the Prince of Wales' Own Regiment of Yorkshire, the Green Howards and the Duke of Wellington's Regiment (West Riding) – that can trace their history back to the 1680s.

The new-look Yorkshire Regiment is made up of three regular army battalions and one Territorial Army battalion, with a total of 2,300 soldiers. Though it sets no limits on its recruitment, the majority of soldiers tend to come from within Yorkshire's historic borders, and the Regiment has a base in Catterick as well as headquarters in York. Its colonel in chief is the Duke of York.

The Regiment – nicknamed the Yorkshire Warriors – wears its Yorkshire connections proudly. It has the white rose on its cap badge, counts several traditional Yorkshire tunes among its regimental music, formally celebrates Yorkshire Day and even has two popular Yorkshire pets, ferrets, as its mascots. It claims to share the county's values of honesty, fairness, pride and hard work, and its motto is 'Fortune Favours the Brave'.

Yorkshire's regiment has been a hardworking one over the years and has seen service recently in Iraq, Afghanistan, Bosnia-Herzegovina and Kosovo. Its men have accumulated 41 Victoria Crosses, eight George Crosses and, since 1695, a total of 280 battle honours. Many of them were awarded during the two world wars, and the regiment chose as its formation day 6 June to coincide with D-Day, in which Yorkshire-based battalions played an important role.

THE DEVIL IN YORKSHIRE

Like many counties in England, Yorkshire's God-fearing past has left it with plenty of sites with connotations with the Devil. Most of the places named after him are associated with local legends; here are five.

The Devil's Apronful. A sprawling cairn of stones on the moor between Nidderdale and Wharfedale. The legend has it that this was the spot where the Devil dropped the stones he was carrying in his apron.

The Devil's Arrows. Three stone monoliths about 20 feet (6 m) high, just off the A1 near Boroughbridge. Thought to be as old as Stonehenge.

The Devil's Bridge. Three arched bridge across the River Lune, technically in Cumbria but regarded as part of the Yorkshire Dales. Devil's Bridges are common across Europe, usually dating from medieval times.

The Devil's Elbow. A hairpin bend on the moor road between Pickering and Whitby.

The Devil's Punchbowl. Also known as the Hole of Horcom, a large, natural amphitheatre on the North York Moors. The legend goes that the Devil scooped out the earth here to create nearby hills.

THE HISTORY OF THE HUMBER BRIDGE

Yorkshire had to wait a long time for a bridge to cross the Humber out of or into the county – but when it finally arrived it was a masterpiece of civil engineering.

Much to the chagrin of people on either side of it, the Humber was the last major unbridged estuary in Britain. As well as being a natural boundary between the counties of Yorkshire on the north bank and Lincolnshire on the south, it had always been a major barrier to transport and trade. For centuries – and probably as far back as Roman times – people and goods were taken across the estuary by boat, and modern-day drivers had a choice between a wait for a slow ferry or a long detour around the estuary. Various schemes to build bridges and tunnels across the estuary were proposed then abandoned, usually because of cost.

The decision to build a suspension bridge between Barton-upon-Humber and Hessle was finally announced by the government in the late 1960s, partly in an effort to secure political support in a marginal seat in Hull. Work didn't begin for several more years, and it wasn't formally opened by the Queen until 1981. The single-span suspension, modelled on the bridge across the Severn, was needed to avoid blocking the Humber with support piers, and while it has since been overtaken by several others, at the time of its opening it was the longest such bridge in the world, stretching for more than a mile (1.6 km) across the estuary.

The bridge has been warmly welcomed by locals, lifted the local economy and substantially reduced motor mileage, especially between ports like Hull and Grimsby – but there are ongoing protests at the steep tolls to cross it. The government replies that they are needed to pay off the bridge's bills. When it was first announced the builder's estimate was £28 million, but escalating construction costs and delays meant that the figure had reached £151 million by the time it was finished. Despite running at a healthy profit, rising interest rates on government loans have since pushed the bill up to a whopping £333 million, and it's not scheduled to be paid off until the 2030s.

The Humber Bridge in numbers

480,000 . . . . .tonnes of concrete used in construction
44,120 . . . . .miles (71,000 km) of wire in the bridge's cables
18,800 .approximate number of vehicles crossing the bridge each day
7,283 . . . . .total length in feet (2,220 m) of the bridge
4,626 . . . . .length in feet (1,410 m) of the largest span
510 . . . . height in feet (155.5 m) of the piers
98 . . . . .height in feet (30 m) above the water
93.5 . . . . .width of the bridge in feet (28.5 m)
80 . . . . .acres (32.4 ha) of painted steelwork
10 . . . . . . .distance in feet (3 m) that the bridge bends in high winds
8 . . . . .years taken to build the bridge

A YORKSHIRE DICTIONARY

Part 1 : A to M

Much imitated but seldom mastered by outsiders, Yorkshire's dialect is one of the most unusual in the country. It has developed over the centuries, drawing on numerous influences from invaders and incomers along the way.

Yorkshire's is also one of the country's most thriving dialects, still widely heard at a time when those in other counties have faded away.

Its vocabulary varies from region to region, and even from village to village, but this list includes some of the more commonly heard words and colloquialisms and their meanings. Not all of them are unique to Yorkshire, of course, but put together they are one of the things that make Yorkshire unique.

aboot – about • afearead – afraid • afooar – before • ah – I •
allus – always • an'all – also • 'appen – perhaps •
atwixt – between • awd – old • awlus – always • aye – yes •
babby – baby • back-end – autumn • badly – poorly •
baht – without • bairn – child • bar – except •
behint – behind • bethink – to remember •
betwaddled – confused, from drink • bewk – book •
bide – to stand, endure • blashy – wet weather •
blether – to talk at length • blowed – surprised •
bobby dazzler – an excellent person • bogie – go-cart •
bonny – attractive • braidy – foolish • brake – broken •
brant – steep • brass – money • bub – to drink • butty – sandwich •
by gum – by God • by heck – by Hell • canny – shrewd, careful •
champion – excellent • chelp – to talk loudly • childer – children •
chuffed – very pleased • chunter – to grumble • clarty – dirty •
clashy – stormy weather • cleas – clothes • clog on – to keep going •
conny – neat, attractive • cop – to catch • dawks – hands •
dee – to die • do – an occasion, event • doff – to take off •
don – to put on • doot – to doubt • dowly – dull, gloomy •
dursn't – dare not • een – eyes • eneeaf – enough •
ey up – look out • faddy – fussy • favver – to resemble •
fettle – condition • feyt – to fight • fizzog – face, physiognomy •
flaid or flait – afraid • flig – to fly • flowtered – excited • fost – first •
fower – four • fra – from • gab – to gossip • galluses – braces •
gan – to go • gannins-on – goings-on • gob – mouth •
grand – excellent • grid – bike • hahse – house • happen – perhaps •
hauf – half • heak – listen to • heeam – home • hissel – himself •
hod – to hold • hoss – horse • hug – to carry • in't – in the •
ivver – ever • jannock – fair, right • jiggered – very tired • jip – pain •
kep – to catch • kersmass – Christmas • kysty – fussy •
laik or laikin – to play • lang – long • lass – girl • latt – late •
leet – light • lewk – look • lish – nimble • lug – to carry •
maddle – to confuse • mardy – miserable • marrer – mate •
mash – to infuse tea • mek – to make • middlin' – moderate •
missel – myself • mithered – irritated • mizzle – mist and drizzle •
monny – many • mullock – to mess around • mun – must

YORKSHIRE SAYINGS

'Give a Yorkshireman a halter and he'll find a horse.'

1974 AND THE END OF YORKSHIRE

Where does Yorkshire start and finish? For centuries its boundaries and identity were quite clear – but since the early 1970s it has all become rather confusing.

Identification with Yorkshire has always varied from region to region and person to person, but the county's borders were traditionally fixed by the three Ridings – a word derived from the Old Norse for third – and, in the middle, the enclave of York. The West, North and East Ridings, measuring 2,770, 2,150 and 1,170 square miles (7,174, 5,568 and 3,030 sq km) respectively, helped to break down the vast span of Yorkshire, and endured invasions, battles and social changes. In 1889 the Ridings were formally recognised as administrative counties for the purposes of local government.

But while the Ridings survived Yorkshire's continuous upheavals, they could not withstand the pens of civil servants. In 1972 a local government act was announced to abolish the administrative counties in favour of metropolitan and non-metropolitan counties, and two years later the changes came into effect. Across the country, out went county names that had been familiar for centuries like Cumberland, Rutland and Westmorland, and in came entirely new entities like Cumbria and Avon.

For Yorkshire it meant the end of the Ridings and the breaking down of the broad acres into a jumble of smaller counties led by south, north and west Yorkshire. Bits of the historic Yorkshire, around the edges in particular, were chipped off and transferred to counties old and new, including Cleveland, Cumbria, Durham, Greater Manchester, Humberside and Lancashire. Towns switched counties overnight – Sedbergh into Cumbria, for instance, and Middlesbrough into Cleveland. To make things even more complicated, the East Riding of Yorkshire returned as a ceremonial county name after a review of the boundaries in the 1990s that also abolished unloved new creations like Cleveland and Avon. Further tinkering with county boundaries since the 1974 act has added to the immense geographical confusion.

How much difference it has all made to people's lives in Yorkshire is a matter of debate. The government insisted that the new regions were for administrative purposes only and that they should not affect people's loyalties to their historical counties. But the changes have certainly ended the stability of the traditional counties that helped people to remember where they came from, and over time they may well dilute Yorkshire's identity.

Either way, the rejigging of boundaries has been studiously ignored by those who acknowledge only the historical borders of the Ridings-divided Yorkshire. The Ridings are still used by many Yorkshire people – both informally in identifying where they live, and formally in many clubs and organisations. The Yorkshire Ridings Society campaigns for the old boundaries, urging people to reject the new counties on their postal addresses in favour of plain 'Yorkshire'. Other pressure groups working to redress the changes include the Association of British Counties, which promotes the use of what it thinks are the 86 traditional counties, and a lively direct action organisation called County Watch, which takes matters into its own hands by moving boundary signs it considers to be in the wrong places.

TEN LONG-DISTANCE WALKS

Yorkshire's wide open spaces are full of great long walks, either completely within its boundaries or just passing through. Here are ten of the most popular trails of 50 miles (80 km) or more, from longest to shortest.

The Pennine Way. A National Trail that takes in a good chunk of Yorkshire and the Dales in particular as it winds between Edale in Derbyshire and Kirk Yetholm on the Scottish borders. An alternative, roughly in parallel, is the Pennine Bridleway. 270 miles (435 km).

The Trans Pennine Trail. From Southport on the Irish Sea to Hull and Hornsea on the North Sea, along disused railways, canal towpaths and other mostly flat paths. On the Yorkshire stretch there are spurs linking the trail to Leeds, York and Sheffield. 215 miles (345 km) from coast to coast and 345 miles (555 km) in all.

Coast to Coast Walk. Devised by Lake District fellwalking legend Alfred Wainwright, from St Bees on the west coast to Robin Hood's Bay on the east. Passes through both the Yorkshire Dales and North York Moors National Parks. 190 miles (306 km).

The Cleveland Way. Along moors and coastline from Helmsley to Filey Brigg, most of it in the North York Moors National Park. 110 miles (177 km).

Lady Anne's Way. From Skipton to Penrith via the Dales, taking in some of the properties and estates of 17th-century landowner Lady Anne Clifford. 100 miles (160 km).

The Dales Way. Scenic route, much of it along riverside paths, from Ilkley in west Yorkshire to Bowness in the Lake District. 80 miles (128 km).

The Yorkshire Wolds Way. From the Humber Bridge through the quiet Wolds down to the coast at Filey. 80 miles (128 km).

The Ebor Way. Through the Vale of York from Helmsley to Ilkley. Takes its name from York's former name of Eboracum. 70 miles (112 km).

The Ribble Way. Linking Lancashire and Yorkshire by following the river from the estuary at Longton near Preston to its source near Ribblehead in the Dales. 70 miles (112 km).

The Nidderdale Way. A circular walk around the Nidd valley, starting and finishing in Hampsthwaite near Harrogate. 55 miles (88 km).

THE YORKSHIRE WHEEL

Yorkshire doesn't like to be outdone by England's capital, so when the London Eye opened in 2000 it didn't take long for the county to come up with an observation wheel of its own.

The Yorkshire Wheel, sited on Leeman Road in York close to the National Railway Museum, started turning in spring 2006 and has been judged a big success. It offers views of the city skyline including York Minster – whose height it rivals – and, on a good day, across Yorkshire. The wheel was initially given permission to run for three years and has already hosted several marriage proposals and weddings. Naturally it has a white rose on its hub.

The Yorkshire Wheel in numbers

3,600,000	cost in pounds
32,500	revolutions in its first year
365	weight in tonnes
177	height in feet (54 m)
164	diameter in feet (50 m)
42	capsules
13	length in minutes of a ride
3	revolutions per ride

YORKSHIRE'S CATHEDRALS

By their definition as the seat of a bishop, Yorkshire has five of the Church of England's 43 cathedrals. They are:

Bradford Cathedral. The oldest parts date from the 15th century, though there is some evidence of prayer on this site as far back as the seventh. It became known as a cathedral from 1919 when a new diocese was created.

Ripon Cathedral. Started by Saint Wilfrid in the 7th century, and his original crypt has survived various rebuildings. Became a cathedral in 1836 and is one of the country's smallest.

Sheffield Cathedral. An Anglo-Saxon cross has provided evidence of worship here for more than a thousand years. Given cathedral status on the creation of the diocese of Sheffield, serving much of south Yorkshire, in 1914.

Wakefield Cathedral. There was probably a wooden church here in Anglo-Saxon times, though the building mostly dates from the 14th and 15th centuries. It was formally turned from a parish church into a cathedral in 1888 and has the highest spire in Yorkshire at 247 feet (75 m).

York Minster. The church dates back to the baptism of King Edwin in 627 and has been continuously added to and repaired. Consecrated as a cathedral in 1472 but has always retained its Minster name.

The Roman Catholic Church has three cathedrals in Yorkshire: Saint Anne's Cathedral in Leeds, completed in 1904; Saint Mary's Cathedral in Middlesbrough, consecrated in 1985; and St Marie's Cathedral in Sheffield, finished in 1850 and a cathedral since 1980.

YORKSHIRE FOOD – YORK'S CHOCOLATE

While other Yorkshire cities and towns built themselves into capitals of various textile industries, York developed a specialism of its own – chocolate.

Though both names are now fading into history after corporate takeovers, Rowntree and Terrys were for a long time among the leading lights in confectionery and hugely important employers in York. Rowntree's history can be traced back to a chocolate shop on

Walmgate in the 18th century, but it wasn't until Henry and Joseph Rowntree took control of the cocoa selling business in the second half of the 19th century that it began to take off. The company originally had a factory by the River Ouse in the centre of York, though production has since moved to various plants on the outskirts. Its list of products – Fruit Pastilles, Walnut Whips, KitKats, Smarties, Aeros, Black Magic and Matchmakers among many more – is a nostalgic trip back to childhood for just about all ages. Terrys' lineage goes back almost as far as its rival, though its name was established only in the 1820s when Joseph Terry took over the Bayldon and Berry company. Its chocolates have included All Gold and Twilight, but it made its name with the Chocolate Orange.

With ports like Hull close at hand to speed the import of cocoa, and an expanding rail network able to distribute products around the country, York was a well-placed capital of confectionery, and Rowntree and Terrys brought economic stability to the city. Both also developed reputations as benevolent employers, introducing benefits and facilities that were unheard of in many of the tough, dangerous factories elsewhere in Yorkshire. But both have changed hands in more recent times, and their new owners have loosened York's grip on the chocolate market. Rowntree first merged with a rival in 1969 to become Rowntree Mackintosh, before being acquired by Nestlé SA in 1988. It has invested in new plants in the city and remains a major employer, but cut several hundred jobs in 2006 after shifting the production of Smarties and other items elsewhere in Europe. The Rowntree name is now largely gone, though it is retained on some of Nestlé's products.

Terrys was meanwhile acquired by food giant Kraft in 1993, and left York for good in 2005 after gradually winding down business in the city. Like Nestlé, Kraft switched production from York's dilapidated Victorian buildings to cheaper and newer plants on the continent, cutting more than 300 jobs in the process – among them members of York families who had worked there for generations. The Terrys factory on Bishopthorpe Road, close to the city's racecourse, is now being redeveloped.

The success of Rowntree and Terrys encouraged other, smaller chocolate manufacturers, both in York and elsewhere in Yorkshire. One of the names that has endured is Thornton's, founded in 1911 when yet another Joseph, Joseph Thornton, opened a chocolate shop in Sheffield.

THE GREAT YORKSHIRE SHOW

The Great Yorkshire Show is the highlight of the agricultural calendar – a three-day celebration of Yorkshire country life and farming that has come a long way in its 170-year history.

After a group of agriculturalists discussed ways of helping the farming industry and rewarding achievements, the show was held for the first time in 1838. That event was staged in York, but the show then toured across Yorkshire to the big towns and agricultural centres. It wasn't until 1950 that the Yorkshire Agricultural Society developed a permanent, 250 acre (100 ha) showground on the edge of Harrogate, where the show has been held ever since, save for in 2001 when an outbreak of foot and mouth disease forced its cancellation. The Harrogate site now hires out space for events all round the year.

Around 6,000 people visited the show in 1842 - the first year for which figures were kept - but these days attendance is well into six figures, reaching a record 135,111 people in 2006. The show now runs over three days from the second Tuesday in July, and is a fascinating mix of agricultural competition and family entertainment. About 10,000 entries a year are received for the vast array of fiercely contested animal classes, drawing farmers from all over Britain and including prestigious titles for the best pig, sheep and cattle of the year. There are demonstrations of animals too, plus marching bands, food and beer tents, flower displays and an important international show-jumping championship called the Cock o'the North.

FAMOUS YORKSHIRE FOLK – THE BRONTËS

On their own, either of Anne, Charlotte and Emily Brontë would usually be ranked among the finest of all novelists - but together they are indisputably the first literary family of Yorkshire, if not of England.

Charlotte's *Jane Eyre*, Emily's *Wuthering Heights* and Anne's *The Tenant of Wildfell Hall* are all still widely read and endlessly adapted for TV or film, and, like their authors, they have their roots firmly in the Yorkshire countryside. All three Brontës were born in Thornton near Bradford - Charlotte in 1816, Emily in 1818 and Anne in 1820 - but moved to Haworth when they were young.

The Brontës endured the death of their mother in 1821, and of two older sisters in 1825. Their father, Patrick, had changed his Irish name from Brunty to the more impressive sounding Brontë, and despite a humble upbringing had become a published author as well as a respected reverend in several parishes across the north. His salary left the Brontës comfortable but never wealthy, but what education the children received was supplemented by lots of reading, writing and talking at home. Together with their only brother Branwell - himself a fair writer - they created imaginary worlds and soaked up ideas for the people, places and stories of their future books from Haworth and its surroundings.

Anne and Charlotte trained to become governesses, which at the time was one of the few career options for women educated enough to be accepted into well-to-do families but without a fortune of their own. They didn't enjoy the work, but all three Brontës kept up their writing and in 1846 used an inheritance to pay for the publication of some of their poems. Though it failed to sell, the next year was the breakthrough one for the sisters, bringing *Jane Eyre*, *Wuthering Heights* and Anne's *Agnes Grey*. Published under the androgynous pseudonyms of Currer, Ellis and Acton Bell, there was immediate speculation about the identity of their authors.

The Brontës didn't have long to enjoy their success. Emily died from tuberculosis the following year, aged just 30 and a few months after Branwell. By now Anne was poorly too, and she died in May 1849 in Scarborough, to where she had gone for a sea cure. Charlotte had lost three siblings in eight months. Returning to her writing, she found her fame spreading and her anonymity disappearing. She published two more novels, *Shirley* and *Villette*, but less than a year after her marriage to a curate of her father's, she too died, in 1855, aged 39. Patrick Brontë had outlived all six of his children, himself dying at Haworth in 1861.

Two years after Charlotte's death, the novelist Elizabeth Gaskell published a biography of her, helping to fan the public's interest in all three Brontë novelists. Their early deaths, leaving only a handful of novels, fuelled Gaskell's image of the trio as brilliant but doomed talents, and the fascination with their lives continues. Haworth receives thousands of Brontë tourists each year, and their first stop is the family's home, now the Brontë Parsonage Museum. But the nearby moors and country houses are just as important to understanding the sisters' work, since much of what they wrote was drawn from observation and developed by imagination. Apart from Anne, who is buried in Scarborough, all the Brontës are interred in the family vault at the church close to the Parsonage in Haworth.

〜〜〜〜〜〜〜〜〜〜〜〜〜〜〜〜〜〜〜

WEATHER LORE

Ten proverbs to help predict the weather, all in circulation in Yorkshire at one time or another and all with dubious basis in meteorology.

Clear moon, frost soon.

If the rain comes before the wind,
Lower your topsails and take them in;
If the wind comes before the rain

Lower your topsails and hoist them again.

The sharper the blast, the sooner it's past.

When the mist comes from the hill,
Then good weather it doth spill;
When the mist comes from the sea.
Then good weather it will be.

If woolly fleeces spread the heavenly way
Be sure no rain disturbs the summer's day.

A red sky at night is the shepherd's delight;
A red sky in the morning is the shepherd's warning.

When the days lengthen, the colds strengthen.

When the sun sets black
A westerly wind will not lack.

A southerly wind with showers of rain
Will bring the wind from west again.

If the cock goes crowing to bed,
He'll certainly rise with a watery head.

A BRIEF HISTORY OF YORK MINSTER

If York is Yorkshire's historic capital, then its Minster is undoubtedly the city's headquarters and focal point. One of the biggest and finest Gothic cathedrals in Europe, it is a treasure trove of religious architecture, stained glass, historical artefacts and, from the tower, some of the best views in Yorkshire.

The Minster – or to give it its full and proper name, the Cathedral and Metropolitan Church of St Peter in York – is also one of the best preserved buildings of its kind and age, though it costs a small fortune to keep it that way, and its history has not exactly been untroubled. Though early records are sketchy, the original Minster is thought to have been a small wooden church built specially for the baptism of Edwin, the Northumbrian Anglo-Saxon king, in 627. It was soon rebuilt in stone and enlarged over the centuries, surviving the era of the Vikings in York relatively unscathed. After it was badly damaged by fire in 1069, the Normans, by now in control of the city, built another stone Minster on the present site that was completed around 1100.

The further rebuilding of the Minster into its current shape began in 1220, and continued at a leisurely pace until it was reconsecrated in 1472. The south and north transepts were added in the 13th century, the nave in the 14th, and the chapel, choir and western towers in the 15th. Though it suffered in the Reformation, and the interior was endlessly adapted to suit the fashions of various times, there were now few major changes to the structure for several hundred years, until two fires – one of them started deliberately by a non-conformist – destroyed roofs in the east end and the nave in 1829. Lightning caused another fire in 1984 that devastated the south transept, prompting four years of restoration. The Minster has undergone a non-stop programme of repair since then, both inside and out, and a joke in the city goes that if the Minster is ever seen without scaffolding then it will be reclaimed by the Catholics. The work of the masons who built the Minster was extraordinary, though their additions to the building weren't always quite properly aligned or structured, and their towers have caused particular headaches over the years, having been identified as on the verge of collapse on several occasions.

The Minster's friendly guides explain more about the history of the building, and though there is now a charge to enter, apart from for services, the money pays for the constant upkeep. Close to a million people now file through each year.

York Minster in numbers

479,001,600 . . . . . . number of different changes in the Minster's bells
895,000 . . . . .annual visitors
1,800 . . . . .approximate number of services held each year
518 . . . . .length in feet (158 m)
415 . . . . .cost in pounds per hour to run the Minster
275 . . . . .steps to the top of the central tower
252 . . . . .years to build the Minster as we largely know it
243 . . . . .width in feet (74 m) at the widest part
197 . . . . .height in feet (60 m) of the central tower
150 . . . . .paid staff looking after the Minster
128 . . . . .stained glass windows, with 2 million pieces of glass
97 . . . . .archbishops of York since 627
17 . . . . .altars
16 . . . . . . .miles (26 km) of scaffolding on the east side, to be removed
in 2016
10 . . . . .serious fires since construction

ENGLAND'S BIGGEST EARTHQUAKE

The sea off Yorkshire was the epicentre of the strongest earthquake ever recorded in Britain in 1931. Measuring 6.1 on the Richter Scale, it occurred in the early hours of 7 June 1931 on the Dogger Bank, about 60 miles (96 km) out to sea from east Yorkshire.

The earthquake was minor by international standards but was felt across the country, with towns along the east coast reporting the biggest impact. A church spire was damaged at Filey, and buildings were rattled elsewhere in Yorkshire, while a minor tidal wave caused floods and stones from the cliffs at Flamborough Head were dislodged. 'All Britain Shaken by an Earthquake,' ran the headline in the *Northern Echo* the next day, 'Alarm in the northeast and people rush from their beds.' Further down it had to add, rather more modestly: 'Little damage and no loss of life.'

YORKSHIRE GRACE

A suitably straightforward and irreverent version of the traditional blessing.

'God bless us all an' make us able,
To eyt all t'stuff 'at's on this table.'

THE YORKSHIRE GIANT

Yorkshiremen and women are fond of saying things are bigger and better in their part of the country than anywhere else - and in one respect at least, they are right.

William Bradley of Market Weighton, a small town between York and Hull, is widely accepted to be the tallest man ever born in Britain. Said to weigh a stone when he was born in 1787 to parents of average height, he grew to 7 feet 9 inches (2.36 m) tall and 27 stones (172 kg) in weight. The title of world's tallest man has since been taken by an American of 8 feet 11 inches (2.7 m), who would have dwarfed even Bradley, but he was an inch or two taller than the current living British record holder. As was common in rather less enlightened times, Bradley was paraded in a travelling circus before returning to live in a specially converted house in Market Weighton, where he died in 1820 aged 32.

Market Weighton has capitalised on its most famous son and record holder with an annual Giant Bradley Day in late May, often attended by modern-day giants. There is also a Giant Bradley Heritage Trail around the town; a plaque to him outside his house on York Road in the shape of one of his giant footprints; and an oak statue – life-size, of course.

SOME ALTERNATIVE YORKSHIRE HEROES

In 2004 the BBC launched a poll to find the greatest ever Yorkshire man or woman. The winner was anti-slavery campaigner William Wilberforce, ahead of explorer Captain James Cook and sculptor Henry Moore in second and third place respectively. But the nominations process also turned up some unlikely 'Yorkshire Greats', including the following dozen.

Sean Bean, actor

Walter Bell, car park attendant at York station

Harry Brearley, inventor of stainless steel

Thomas Crapper, inventor of the toilet

Def Leppard, rock band

Kelly Fisher, snooker player

Paul Hudson, weather forecaster

David Jefferies, motorcyclist

Michael Parkinson, TV personality

Dennis Priestley, darts player

Diana Rigg, actress

Patrick Stewart, actor

THE BATTLEFIELDS OF YORKSHIRE

From Viking invaders to skirmishes with the Scots to the Wars of the Roses to the Civil War, Yorkshire's history is notably bloody. Each of its battles tells part of the county's story, and many of the battlefields are sufficiently preserved to give a decent impression of the encounters.

Here are ten key battles fought in Yorkshire between the 11th and 17th centuries.

Battle of Fulford. In which Viking King Harald Hardrada overcame the forces of the Earls Morcar and Edwin to secure York in 1066.

Battle of Stamford Bridge. Where Harold successfully fought off Hardrada a few days after Fulford and three weeks before the Battle of Hastings. It was the first time a foreign invader had been defeated in Britain. The village, close to York, has a memorial stone and a pub called the Swordsman Inn.

Battle of the Standard. A battle fought at Cowton Moor, north of Northallerton, between English and Scottish forces in 1138. Sometimes known as the Battle of Northallerton. Ten thousand men were killed, and there is a monument on the A167.

Battle of Myton. A brief, bloody clash in the Scottish War of Independence in 1319, between tough Scottish forces and disorganised Yorkshire militia. The exact spot around the current village of Myton-on-Swale near Boroughbridge is unknown.

Battle of Boroughbridge. A short but famous 1322 battle that saw the men of Edward I defeat the rebel forces of his uncle, the Earl of Lancaster. A plaque on the town's bridge remembers the battle.

Battle of Wakefield. A key Roses battle between Yorkists and Lancastrians in 1460 that killed thousands and saw the red rose triumph. The site is just to the west of Sandal Castle.

Battle of Towton. The biggest of all the Yorkist-Lancastrian encounters and – with Marston Moor – one of the biggest of all battles on British soil, fought a year after Wakefield in 1461. It killed tens of thousands of men. One of the combatants, Lord Dacres, is buried at Saxton churchyard.

Battle of Seacroft Moor. Where the Royalists saw off Thomas Fairfax's Parliamentarians in 1643. Seacroft is a few miles east of Leeds.

Battle of Adwalton Moor. Another Civil War skirmish involving Fairfax's men that he came close to winning but that consolidated the Royalists' control of the north. The site is close to Bradford.

Battle of Marston Moor. Civil War battle of 1644 between the Royalists and the Parliamentarian army. The battle was important in determining control of the north and enhanced the reputation of the Parliamentarians' commander, Oliver Cromwell.

YORKSHIRE'S MEANEST MAN AND WOMAN

Yorkshire's reputation as a place where people are particularly careful with money is largely without foundation as a rule - with one or two exceptions.

The stereotype of the tight Yorkshireman is at least partly drawn from Old John Mealy-Face, a man from Topcliffe in north Yorkshire whose way with money was legendary. His nickname was drawn from his habit of pressing his face into the flour bin before he went out so that he could tell if the impression had been disturbed when he came back - either by locals stealing the flour or his wife using it to bake bread without his permission.

John's female equivalent, who died not long after he was born towards the end of the 18th century, was Margaret Wharton. Living at Skelton Castle and having inherited the vast sum of £200,000, she became renowned among traders throughout Yorkshire for buying items only in the smallest possible quantities, attracting the nickname Peg Pennyworth. She also insisted on sampling large quantities of everything before she bought, and on being asked for a donation to charity supposedly sifted through a ream of notes before handing over one of the lightest. She was the subject of a play by a satirist of the time, which she is said to have hugely enjoyed. She is buried at York Minster.

THE YORKSHIRE HUNTS

No 21st-century law has stirred up Yorkshire as much as the ban on hunting with dogs, passed after months of political wrangling in 2004. For hunts across Yorkshire it brought to an end centuries of tradition and, they argue, diminished the county's character.

Yorkshire fox hunting, in which trained hounds follow the scent of their prey with horses and their riders in hot pursuit, dates back to at least the mid-17th century. That's the point to which the Bilsdale hunt in the North York Moors can trace its history, making it the longest established fox hunt in the country. There was sadness and anger at Bilsdale and the dozen or so other Yorkshire hunt headquarters when the ban was introduced, and while it was warmly welcomed by campaigners against blood sports, it has caused outrage among many rural communities, unhappy that London politicians had put an end to centuries of countryside tradition.

Both sides of the debate would probably acknowledge that the actual chasing and killing of foxes is less important than the traditions that have grown up around the hunts. The dress code, hierarchy and social rituals of the hunt are all much loved by supporters, though they have probably helped the argument of critics that it is a preserve of the landed gentry - when, in Yorkshire at least, riders have in fact been increasingly drawn from across the classes.

The ban has undoubtedly changed hunting, the season for which runs from late October to late March or early April. Bilsdale and other hunts have tried to carry on their activities within the new laws by simply leading their hounds on trails - often under the watchful eyes of anti-hunt activists making sure they don't pursue foxes. Some hunts claim that outrage at the ban has made them more popular than ever among both riders and new supporters, and are determined to keep their activities going until they can force a repeal of the act.

BRITAIN'S BEST WALK

According to a survey by *Country Walking* magazine, Britain's best walk is the Coast to Coast trail between the North and Irish Seas, passing through the breadth of Yorkshire along the way.

The Coast to Coast walk was devised in 1973 by Alfred Wainwright, best known for his classic books on the Lake District but who also enjoyed walking throughout Yorkshire. His route sets off from St Bees Head near Whitehaven on the western coast and takes in several Cumbrian fells and valleys before entering Yorkshire east of Kirkby Stephen and finishing up at Robin Hood's Bay on the coast. It measures around 190 miles (305 km), though it was never meant to be a prescriptive trail, and the many different variations on Wainwright's route can increase or reduce the distance.

The walk passes through two of Yorkshire's National Parks - the Yorkshire Dales and the North York Moors - and winds pleasantly through the county's dales, fells, moors and varied scenery. The walking is mostly straightforward, though the distance is considerable and the climbs and exposure on some high parts - most of them over the border in Cumbria - are not to be taken lightly. The route passes through a few sizeable towns, like Kirkby Stephen and Richmond, but it mostly steers around them, instead bringing the tourist business of walkers to otherwise quiet places.

Most people walk the route from west to east so as to have the wind at their backs, and guidebooks generally suggest taking a fortnight over it, breaking the distance down into chunks of 10 to 15 miles

(16–24 km) a day. Some walkers take years over it, walking stretches on occasional weekends – and naturally others have competed to complete it as quickly as possibly, the record currently standing at a little under 40 hours. Despite being one of the most popular long-distance walks in the country, the route has not yet been designated as an official National Trail, meaning that signposting is not always clear. But on summer weekends it's usually possible to follow others on the same mission, and the popularity of the walk means that paths are being badly eroded in places.

As well as naming it Britain's best, *Country Walking*'s poll also put the Coast to Coast route second on the list of best walks in the world. The top walk, the Milford Track, is a little further off – in New Zealand.

YORKSHIRE'S NATIONAL NATURE RESERVES

Natural England looks after England's National Nature Reserves – sites with important wildlife or geology that need extra protection from potential damage. Of the 200 or so reserves in the country, Yorkshire has ten. They are:

Duncombe Park. Ancient woodlands plus some rare species in and around the River Rye, all in the grounds of a country house near Helmsley.

Forge Valley Woods. Deciduous woodlands, named after a forge that used to stand nearby.

Humberhead Peatlands. Some 7,410 acres (3,000 ha) of raised bogs support about 5,000 species of plants and animals.

Ingleborough. There are about 2,470 acres (1,000 ha) of limestone pavements in the Yorkshire Dales, with some unique wildlife.

Lower Derwent Valley. Meadows, pastures and woodlands with 80 or so species of birds.

Ling Gill. Limestone gorge with various micro-climates, not usually accessible to the public.

Malham Tarn. Large tarn in the Dales with some rare species, and limestone pavements close by.

New House Farm. Traditionally maintained working Dales farm with some rare hay meadows, near Malham Tarn.

Scoska Wood. Ash woodland in the Littondale valley.

Spurn. Peninsula near the mouth of the Humber, taking in sandy beaches, saltmarshes and mudflats.

YORKSHIRE ARTISTS

Here are 15 of Yorkshire's most famous painters, sculptors and photographers, together with their place of birth.

Kenneth Armitage (1916–2002) – Leeds
Doug Binder (b.1941) – Bradford
Henry Dawson (1811–78) – Hull
William Etty (1787–1849) – York
John Flaxman (1755–1826) – York
John Atkinson Grimshaw (1836–93) – Leeds
Barbara Hepworth (1903–75) – Wakefield
Patrick Heron (1920–99) – Leeds
David Hockney (b.1937) – Bradford
John Hoyland (b.1934) – Sheffield
William Kent (1685–1748) – Bridlington
Percy Metcalfe (1895–1970) – Wakefield
Henry Moore (1898–1986) – Castleford
Frank Meadow Sutcliffe (1853–1941) – Whitby
Henry Scott Tuke (1858–1929) – York

YORKSHIRE'S HOME-GROWN CRICKETERS

Yorkshire's county cricket team was one of the most dominant of all British sporting sides throughout the 20th century – and until very recently it could say its success was entirely home-grown.

For 129 years from the club's formation in 1863, Yorkshire stuck rigidly to a policy of only selecting players born within the historic county borders. It showed both Yorkshire's pride in its history and the large supply of sporting talent within its boundaries – as well, perhaps, as a stubborn belief that the county was England's cricket capital. The policy is one of the things that has given Yorkshire its self-confidence and sense of being a distinct country within a country.

And it served them well, since the club won 30 county championships in just 75 years, including seven in the 1930s and six in the 1960s. But in the 1970s, as other counties began to sign up overseas players and tempt some of its own players away, Yorkshire found its supremacy challenged. In 1992, more than two decades after its last county championship win, the club decided to amend its famous rule to include those who had been educated within Yorkshire as well as those born there – thus accommodating the future England captain Michael Vaughan, born over the Pennines in Salford but brought up in Yorkshire. Soon afterwards it abandoned the policy altogether, legendary Indian batsman Sachin Tendulkar becoming the first Yorkshire player to have been born overseas. Whether it was done in recognition of the changing times or because it was desperate for success again, the move was met with howls of anguish from Yorkshire patriots. But within a decade of the change Yorkshire was again celebrating a county championship.

ON THE TRAIL OF ALL CREATURES GREAT AND SMALL

Just as the land around Haworth is so closely linked with Anne, Charlotte and Emily Brontë that it is now known as Brontë Country, so a wedge of north Yorkshire has been adopted as Herriot Country.

James Herriot is Yorkshire and England's most famous ever vet. In real life he was Alf Wight, born in Sunderland in 1916 and an adopted Yorkshireman from the day he joined the Kirkgate practice in Thirsk in 1940. After spending years on call to farmers across the Dales and North York Moors, he was persuaded by his wife to write up his anecdotes, borrowing the Herriot pen-name from a footballer he had seen on television. His first book, *If Only They Could Talk*, was published in 1970, and his easygoing, humorous and affectionate snapshots of rural Yorkshire life struck chords well beyond the borders of Yorkshire, finding a substantial market in the US in particular. Several more books followed, mixing real-life stories with fiction. They were adapted into two feature films in the mid-1970s, and a few years later the BBC began a hugely popular series adapting the books over more than 80 episodes, spreading Herriot's reputation even wider.

Though the TV series ended in the early 1990s and Wight died in 1995, the books still sell well, and the shows are endlessly repeated on satellite channels. Few individuals have done as much for Yorkshire tourism as Herriot, and his old stomping ground in and around Thirsk draws visitors from around the world. The focal point is his old surgery in Thirsk, a town known as Darrowby in print and on screen. The building was bought by the district council after Wight's death and has been nicely restored to how it would have looked in the 1940s and

1950s. It is now branded as the World of James Herriot and open all year round, with serious displays on veterinary science as well as TV memorabilia, like Herriot's Austin car. The original TV set has ended up at the Richmondshire Museum in Richmond.

Thirsk has other Herriot connections – the Golden Fleece Hotel, for instance, is the real-life Drovers Arms from the books and TV programmes. Tours are available of various Herriot sites in the Dales, and an annual Herriot Convention offers excursions and lectures. There is even a Herriot Way, a 55 mile (88 km) circular trail starting and finishing in Aysgarth and taking in much of the territory he covered as a vet.

SOME UNUSUAL PUB NAMES

Among the ubiquitous pub names – the Crowns, Red Lions, Royal Oaks, Swans and so on – Yorkshire has a handful of inns with weird and wonderful titles, often handed down through the centuries. Here are twenty of the strangest.

The Bottom House, Whitby • The Chemic Tavern, Leeds •
The Cod and Lobster, Staithes • The Cottage of Content, Rotherham •
The Dotterel, Reighton • The Falling Stone, Thwing •
The Mucky Duck Inn, Pickering • The Needless Inn, Morley •
The Noose and Gibbet, Sheffield • The Old Silent Inn, Stanbury •
The One Eyed Rat, Ripon • The Shoulder of Mutton, York •
The Slubbers Arms, Huddersfield • The Spangled Bull, Dewsbury •
The Squinting Cat, Harrogate • The Three Jolly Sailors, Burniston •
The Three Legged Mare, York • The Turkey Inn, Goose Eye •
The Tut 'n' Shive, Bradford • The Wasps Nest, Mirfield

UNDERGROUND YORKSHIRE

The limestone running through the Yorkshire Dales makes it an outstanding place for caving and potholing.

Cave networks here are the biggest and most extensive in the country, some winding underground for dozens of miles. Popular systems include Gaping Gill, Mossdale Caverns, the White Scar caves and Ingleborough cave, and a handful are open to the public as 'show' caves – a good option if you want to explore underground under guidance but don't fancy getting too wet or dirty. Ingleton, the caving capital of Yorkshire, is a good place to get started, and there are several clubs across the county that are usually happy to take beginners along on trips to – quite literally – show them the ropes.

The caves of the Dales vary enormously in shape, size and condition, from cramped, flooded holes to vast open spaces, and they are also important habitats for bats, butterflies, moths and insects. Though accidents are rare, the risks of floods, getting lost or – occasionally – getting stuck can make it dangerous, and voluntary rescue teams like the Clapham-based Cave Rescue Organisation and the Upper Wharfedale Fell Rescue Association are permanently on call to assist.

YORKSHIRE FOOD – RHUBARB

Yorkshire once produced 90 per cent of the world's forced rhubarb crop, and although it has faced competition from overseas in the last few years, it is still one of the area's biggest food treasures and a popular export.

Rhubarb was first brought to Britain in the 16th century, and it was used for medicinal purposes long before it went into crumbles, foods and other puddings. Through the 19th century production began to focus on the 'Rhubarb Triangle', a patch of Yorkshire between Wakefield, Leeds and Bradford. The cold, damp soil of the area was found to be ideal for rhubarb, and the by-products of nearby industries are thought to have had a fertilising effect on it, making for excellent conditions. As its reputation spread, several hundred producers, mostly very small scale, were growing rhubarb, and in its heyday it was being dispatched by specially chartered trains down to London and on across the country.

'Forcing' rhubarb is done by growing it in artificially darkened conditions – a technique discovered, as many seem to be, by accident – and the process is something of a ritual in Yorkshire. Having been outdoors for two years, the roots of rhubarb are brought into pitch dark sheds at the end of the year and kept warm and moist. Here, the rhubarb stems reach upwards looking for light, and within a few weeks the vivid pink-red stalks are ready to be picked. This is done by candlelight to protect the stalks that are still growing – and by hand, since this is one of the few faming processes that cannot be mechanised. The forced rhubarb season usually lasts until March, when the outdoor version is used instead – though most people agree that Yorkshire's indoor rhubarb is far superior in taste, being sweeter and more succulent. Growers attract tourists curious to see the candlelit harvesting, and Wakefield hosts a Rhubarb Festival each March to promote the crop.

Rising costs, cheap imports and problems with image caused by overcooked, bitter rhubarb in school dinners has caused the number of producers to dwindle. But a revival of interest in local food and some welcome publicity about the health benefits of rhubarb have helped the handful of remaining producers lately, and rhubarb has become a fashionable ingredient in savoury as well as sweet dishes. The producers' plight will be helped further if they are successful in their ongoing efforts to secure protected status for their rhubarb. Just as Parma Ham, Arbroath Smokies and Newcastle Brown Ale enjoy protection from rivals trying to imitate their product, so Yorkshire Indoor Rhubarb might soon be restricted to the Wakefield triangle that has made it so famous.

A recipe for rhubarb fool
450 g forced Yorkshire rhubarb
150 g granulated sugar
284 ml double cream

Trim the rhubarb of its ends and chop the stalks into medium sized chunks. Put the rhubarb in a pan with half the sugar and a few tablespoons of water. Cook over a low heat for about 10 minutes or until the rhubarb is tender. Stir in the rest of the sugar – or to taste – and leave to cool. Whisk the cream into soft peaks. Strain the juice from the rhubarb mixture into the cream and whisk again briefly. Now fold in the rhubarb, leaving a few pieces aside. Spoon the mixture into wine glasses or small pots and place the spare rhubarb pieces on top. You could stir in a few tablespoons of Cointreau or similar at the whisking stage if you want to give the fool a bit of a kick.

HOW TO WORK OUT YORKSHIRE'S WIND CHILL

When the wind whips up on Yorkshire's exposed fells and moors, the temperature can seem a good deal lower than the weather forecast promised. This is the wind chill – the temperature that is felt on exposed skin rather than the air measurement. Lots of different methods have been used to measure and index wind chill, but the formula currently used by the Met Office is as follows.

$$Wind\ Chill = 35.74 + 0.6215T - 35.75(V^{0.16}) + 0.4275(V^{0.16})$$

Where T is the air temperature in ° Fahrenheit and V is the wind speed in miles per hour

This table shows the wind chill according to the air temperature and wind. With an air temperature of 30°F (-1°C) and wind of 40 mph (64 kph), for instance, the wind chill is 13°F (-10°C). Frostbite can set in in less than 30 minutes if the wind chill falls beneath -18°F (-28°C). So wrap up warm.

Wind in mph (kph)

Air temp in °F (°C)	10 (16)	20 (32)	30 (48)	40 (64)	50 (80)	60 (96)
50 (10)	46 (8)	44 (7)	42 (6)	41 (5)	40 (4.5)	39 (4)
40 (4)	34 (1)	30 (-1)	28 (-2)	27 (-3)	26 (-3.5)	25 (-4)
30 (-1)	21 (-6)	17 (-8)	15 (-9)	13 (-10)	12 (-11)	10 (-12)
20 (-7)	9 (-13)	4 (-16)	1 (-17)	-1 (-18)	-3 (-19)	-4 (-20)

FAMOUS YORKSHIRE FOLK –
WILLIAM WILBERFORCE

Few Yorkshiremen have had so important an effect on the wider world as William Wilberforce, and a recent BBC poll to find the leading 'Yorkshire Greats' placed him above even Captain James Cook at the top of the pile.

Wilberforce was by no means the only man to work for the ending of the slave trade, but his is the name that has come to be most commonly associated with the abolition movement. He was born into a rich Yorkshire merchant family in Hull in 1759 and became seriously interested in social reform after converting to something of an evangelical Christian in his twenties. By this time he was member of parliament for his home town and, after meeting abolitionists including Thomas Clarkson, he began to campaign for an end to slavery through parliamentary bills and literature for the public.

Supported by Prime Minister William Pitt the Younger, a university friend, Wilberforce became the unofficial parliamentary leader of the abolition movement, tenaciously keeping the issue on the political agenda and speaking eloquently in its support. His efforts were frustrated by parliamentary delaying tactics and wars with France, but he refused to give up on his campaign. Trading in slaves in the British Empire was abolished by law in 1807, and Wilberforce was cheered to the rafters in the House of Commons - though it wasn't until 1833, a matter of days before his death, that existing slaves were finally freed.

Wilberforce was a man ahead of his time, and he championed other social reforms, including the improvement of factory conditions, charity schools, a halt to cruelty to animals and various Christian missions overseas, especially to formerly enslaved countries. But in other respects he was something of a conservative, fighting various forms of immorality through the Society of Suppression of Vice. Wilberforce is buried alongside Pitt in London's Westminster Abbey, but is remembered with affection throughout Yorkshire too. Hull is particularly proud of its connections, and his birthplace is marked by a monument and the Wilberforce House Museum, recently refurbished to mark the bicentenary of the abolition of the slave trade. And in 2007, another prominent Yorkshire politician, former Conservative leader William Hague, published a very good biography of Wilberforce.

YORKSHIRE'S ULTIMATE CRICKET TEAM?

Picking a fantasy cricket team from across the ages is a popular pursuit for Yorkshire cricket followers. This line-up is based purely on numbers rather than opinions about relative merits, but it's nonetheless a formidable side. It includes the six highest run scorers in the history of the club, and – since two of them are all-rounders – the six highest wicket takers too. Plus the wicket-keeper with the most catches and stumpings too, of course.

The side is dominated by players from the late 19th and early 20th centuries, when Yorkshire sides played much more cricket than they do now and players had a greater chance of accumulating runs and wickets. The only two players from after the Second World War are Geoff Boycott and Fred Trueman. And while Yorkshire supporters might argue endlessly over the omissions from this side, they can't argue with its purity – all eleven were born and bred in Yorkshire.

1 Herbert Sutcliffe (38,558 runs for Yorkshire)

2 Percy Holmes (26,220 runs)

3 Geoff Boycott (32,570 runs)

4 David Denton (33,282 runs)

5 George Hirst (32,035 runs and 2,477 wickets)

6 Wilfred Rhodes (31,098 runs and 3,597 wickets)

7 David Hunter (913 catches and 350 stumpings)

8 Schofield Haigh (1,876 wickets)

9 George Macauley (1,774 wickets)

10 Fred Trueman (1,745 wickets)

11 Hedley Verity (1,158 wickets)

FOOT AND MOUTH IN YORKSHIRE

Yorkshire's farmers have faced plenty of challenges over the last few decades, but none quite as traumatic as the outbreak of foot mouth disease in 2001.

Though Cumbria bore the brunt of the outbreak, the northern half of Yorkshire was hard hit too, and as the disease spread like wildfire through Britain in the spring, the farming community was decimated. Affected livestock was slaughtered and piled in grim mass burial sites, and restrictions on movement sealed off farms. By the time the region was finally declared foot and mouth free in December 2001, Yorkshire had recorded 139 confirmed outbreaks of the disease – the fourth highest of any county behind Cumbria, Dumfries and Galloway and Devon. Animals on infected farms had to be slaughtered without delay, but the need to contain the spread meant that culls were also in place on about four times as many farms. More than 50,000 cattle and 300,000 sheep were slaughtered in Yorkshire, and across the country more than 6 million animals were culled.

The crisis had an enormous financial impact. At its peak, Yorkshire's rural economy was slashed by almost a fifth, and UK-wide it was estimated to have cost the public and private sectors £3 billion and £5 billion respectively. The crisis spread way beyond the farm gates in Yorkshire, closing auction markets and forcing the cancellation of agricultural shows, some of which had been running continuously for decades. It had a massive effect on tourism too. Over-the-top media coverage gave the false impression that the countryside was completely out of bounds, and visits to many of the dales dried up overnight. Rural businesses, including hotels and pubs, saw takings plummet, and a report into the outbreak estimated that tourism in the Yorkshire and Humber region lost around £125 million in the first three months of the crisis. There were 100,000 fewer trips a month as a direct result of the crisis, with the number of overseas visitors particularly affected.

Other impacts of foot and mouth were impossible to measure. The psychological effect on rural communities was immense, and even though farmers were compensated for their slaughtered livestock, the distress and anxiety caused by the outbreak were enough to prompt many to leave the farming or tourism industries. There was also widespread anger at the delays in the official handling of the crisis, something criticised by several reports in subsequent years.

Gradually, however, some good came out of the disaster. Emergency funding safeguarded many jobs, and money for a big marketing campaign helped to bring in tourists once foot and mouth had been cleared. Many farmers and tourist businesses were prompted to think about diversification and developed new strings to their bows, like bed and breakfast or farm shops. Lessons from the handling of the crisis seem to have been learned too. While there have since been further foot and mouth scares causing movement restrictions and the cancellations of some county shows, there has, fortunately, been nothing to match the catastrophic events of 2001.

DICK TURPIN'S YORKSHIRE END

Fact and fiction are hard to distinguish in the life of Dick Turpin, but it is clear that the country's most famous highwayman met his end in Yorkshire.

Victorian ballads and modern films have romanticised Turpin somewhat over the years, and he was in all probability a much more brutal and ruthless villain than the popular image of dashing, roguish hero would have us believe. He was born in Essex and conducted most of the robbery that made his reputation around London, dealing more in animal rustling, torture and probably murder than in the stick-ups of the wealthy that the legends suggest.

When the game was finally up and Turpin fled from London for Yorkshire, he did so in a famously fast ride on his legendary horse Black Bess along what is now the A1 – though some historians doubt it ever happened. He certainly ended up in Yorkshire, setting up as a horse dealer by the name of John Palmer and usually trading in animals he had himself stolen. He was finally arrested after shooting the rooster of the landlord of an inn he was staying in near Brough, after which his true identity was discovered. He was hanged on the Knavesmire in York in 1739. Turpin was buried in St George's churchyard in York, and while his body is thought to have been dug up soon afterwards, a headstone there remembers him. Elsewhere in the city, York Castle Museum has recreated the cell where he spent his last night before his execution.

19TH-CENTURY YORKSHIRE OCCUPATIONS

The Yorkshire census of 1861 reveals the top ten professions of the time. It's interesting to note how many of these jobs have now disappeared altogether.

1 Labourer

2 Servant

3 Worsted weaver/spinner

4 Coal miner

5 Dressmaker

6 Housekeeper

7 Carter

8 Woollen weaver

9 Tailor

10 Stone mason

SOME DAFT SURVEY FINDINGS

Few days pass without the media relaying the findings of yet another spurious survey into aspects of British life. Some provide interesting insights into regional differences, though most are thinly disguised plugs for whoever has carried out the survey. One recent poll, for instance, 'discovered' that Yorkshire gave visitors a friendlier welcome than any other part of the country. Who conducted it? Yorkshire Tourist Board. Here are ten more things we have learned from surveys.

Yorkshire has the most dangerous pavements. A third of pavements in the Yorkshire and Humber region are in need of repair, compared to one in four nationwide. Each year 2.5 million people over the age of 65 fall over on pavements. (Source: Chartered Society of Physiotherapy)

Yorkshire is Britain's psychic capital. The county has more people claiming psychic powers or to have had close encounters of the third kind than any other. (Source: SciFi TV)

Yorkshire has the worst public toilets. Only 18 per cent of people in Yorkshire and the Humber were pleased with their facilities, the lowest figure in Britain. (Source: National Consumer Council)

Yorkshire people are most likely to pick up money in the street. 70 per cent of people living in the Yorkshire and Humber region said they would pick up a penny if they saw it, compared to a regional low of 41 per cent in London. Britons find an average of £4 in loose change each year. (Source: fool.co.uk)

Yorkshire is the most obese county in Britain. It has three of the top ten overweight cities – Bradford, Sheffield and Leeds. (Source: Men's Fitness)

Yorkshire people have the most friends. Residents have an average of 15.4 close friends, three more than the next ranking region and three times the number of London residents. (Source: Ocean View)

Yorkshire has England's best doctors. Based on quality of care, waiting times, outcomes and patients' opinions, the west Yorkshire region scored higher than any other. (Source: NHS Quality and Outcomes Framework)

Yorkshire has the most rats in England. Increased litter and reduced budgets for pest control are to blame. (Source: National Pest Technicians Association)

Yorkshire people enjoy Christmas least. Only 15 per cent of Yorkshire residents said they fully enjoyed Christmas, the lowest proportion in the country. (Source: Matthew Walker Ltd)

Yorkshire has the happiest workers. 59 per cent of people working in Yorkshire said they were very happy with their current jobs and had no desire to change, more than in any other part of Britain. (Source: YouGov)

TOP DOG

The terrier may be Yorkshire's most famous breed of dog, but the single most famous animal to have come out of the county is undoubtedly Lassie.

Her creator, Eric Mowbray Knight, was born not in Hollywood as most Americans assume but in Menston in west Yorkshire in 1897. His family was fairly affluent, but when his father abandoned them Eric took work in a spinning mill in Halifax. When he was 15 his mother remarried and took him to live in the US, and after serving with the Canadian army in the First World War he returned there to work as a journalist, film critic and scriptwriter. Knight became a prolific author, setting some of his books in Yorkshire, but he is now remembered almost solely for a story about a boy and his dog that was first published in 1938. *Lassie Come Home* was originally a short piece written for a newspaper, but its popularity soon prompted a book and then a film, for which Knight himself wrote the screenplay in 1942. A year later, while serving again in the army, he was killed in a mysterious plane crash in the jungle of Dutch Guinea, now Surinam.

Lassie's story has firm Yorkshire roots, even if it has been sentimentalised and Americanised out of all recognition over the years. America's screen adaptations have put Lassie in the wilds of California or the Midwest, but Knight had set his story of triumph over adversity in a bleak Yorkshire mining town. He had revisited his home county in the hard times of the 1930s, when some families were forced to sell their dogs to buy food, and he took the idea with him back home to America. After being sold many hundreds of miles away in Scotland, Knight's Lassie finds his way back to Yorkshire and her devoted young owner – encountering lots of exciting adventures along the way, of course. The bond between dog and boy was based on Knight's own pet, a Collie.

The original film was filmed and financed in Hollywood, something that made its Yorkshire setting rather unconvincing. Nevertheless, it was hugely popular, spawning endless movie remakes, dozens more books and a TV series that ran for an incredible 600 or so episodes. Seventy years on, Lassie is probably the most famous animal ever seen on screen, and her pawprints are alongside the handprints of Hollywood greats on the famous pavement of Sunset Boulevard. She has come a long way from Knight's Yorkshire dog story.

THE THANKFUL VILLAGES

Of the thousands of villages across England, just 32 could claim to be 'Thankful Villages' – to which all the men from there who fought in the First World War returned after its conclusion in 1918. The list was drawn up by Arthur Mee in his *King's England* guide to the counties of England in the 1930s. He identified four such villages in Yorkshire.

Catwick, northeast of Beverley
Cundall, east of Ripon
Norton-le-Clay, east of Ripon
Scruton, west of Northallerton

Subsequent research by historians after Mee suggests that **Helperthorpe**, east of Malton, can also claim to be a 'Thankful Village'.

THE PEAK DISTRICT IN NUMBERS

Some facts and figures about the Peak District National Park.

22,000,000	annual visitor days
202,000	average house price in pounds in 2006
37,937	population living within the boundaries
17,916	household spaces
5,440	miles (8,755 km) of dry stone walls
2,896	listed buildings
2,086	highest point in feet (636 m) – Kinder Scout
1951	year the National Park was established
1,867	miles (3,005 km) of public rights of way
555	area in square miles (1,437 sq km) of the National Park
430	scheduled ancient monuments
233	square miles (603 sq km) of improved pasture
178	square miles (461 sq km) of heath or moorland
125	parishes
109	conservation areas
68	residents per square mile (2.6 sq km)
55	reservoirs
52	sites of Special Scientific Interest
44	square miles (114 sq km) of woodland
40	approximate inches (1,025 mm) average of rainfall per year
35	percentage of land defined as 'open access'
15	percentage of the park area within Yorkshire
3.6	percentage of the park population within Yorkshire
1	National Nature Reserve

THE TYKE'S MOTTO

Tyke was once a common nickname for Yorkshire people, its use probably deriving from its definition as a dog of the terrier type that was widely owned in the county. It is used these days with more affection than was probably the case when it was first coined and serves as the nickname of Barnsley Football Club. The source of the Tyke's Motto - sometimes also known as the Yorkshireman's Creed - is unknown, but it is endlessly reprinted on tea towels for tourists. (Allus is Yorkshire dialect for always; thysen for yourself.)

See all, hear all, say nowt,
Eat all, sup all, pay nowt;
And if tha does owt for nowt
Allus do it for thysen.

❧❧ ❧❧ ❧❧ ❧❧ ❧❧ ❧❧ ❧❧ ❧❧ ❧❧ ❧❧ ❧❧

TEN CASTLES

Yorkshire's colourful history has left it with plenty of castles and other fortified buildings in various stages of preservation. Excluding castles like Castle Howard or Bolton Castle, which were built primarily as private residences, here are ten of the best that are open to the public. Unless otherwise stated the castles are looked after by English Heritage.

Conisbrough Castle. A castle was first built here soon after the Norman Conquest. The remains of the later stone building are now overlooked by a tall, unusually cylindrical 12th-century keep. It was the inspiration for Walter Scott's novel *Ivanhoe*.

Helmsley Castle. Atmospheric Norman castle with banks and ditches all around and overlooking the town. It was the site of a three-month siege by Parliamentarians during the Civil War.

Middleham Castle. Richard III's childhood home, a fortified palace with a huge 12th-century keep. Though the roofs have long gone, the layout of the castle is well preserved.

Pickering Castle. A motte and bailey castle on the edge of the North York Moors, built with timber just after the Norman Conquest and later enforced by stone. An exhibition is attached.

Pontefract Castle. There are very few remains of the castle now, but it was once among the most important fortresses in the country. Originally built after the Norman Conquest, it was destroyed during the Civil War. Now looked after by Wakefield district council.

Richmond Castle. Perched above the River Swale, this is one of the oldest stone castles in the country. Much of it is very well preserved, especially the 12th-century keep. Conscientious objectors were held here during the First World War.

Sandal Castle. There are very few remains of the motte and bailey castle, but the surrounding site has been well excavated. Finds can be seen at a visitor centre, owned - like the castle and the one at Pontefract - by Wakefield district council. The Battle of Wakefield in the Wars of the Roses was fought close by in 1460.

Scarborough Castle. With a spectacular location on the cliffs above Scarborough and the sea, this spot has been used as a fortress and look-out point for some 2,500 years. The keep was built by Henry II.

Skipton Castle. Small medieval castle but one of the best preserved anywhere in the country, still lived in though widely open to the public. It was under siege for three years during the Civil War.

York Castle (Clifford's Tower). Most of the castle is long gone, but the keep has survived nearly a thousand years since being built by William the Conqueror. It is named after Roger de Clifford, hanged there for treason in 1322.

A GUIDE TO THE GHOSTS OF YORK

Whether it's because of its long history of conflict and tragedy or because of an inspired marketing campaign, York is often considered to be the ghost capital of England. The Ghost Research Foundation even considers it to be the most haunted city in the world, with more than 500 'recorded hauntings' – whatever that means.

If all the claims are to be believed, ghosts haunt just about every other building or street in York, and they help to keep dozens of ghost hunters, tour guides and storytellers in business. There is an annual York Ghost Festival, scheduled, naturally enough, in the run-up to Hallowe'en, and ghost-hunting events run by the enterprising tourist board. The dark, ancient streets lend themselves very well to some atmospheric tours, and there are several ghost walks to choose from most nights, including the Ghost Trail of York (tel. 01904 633276 or visit www.ghostrail.co.uk); the Ghost Hunt of York (tel. 01904 608700 or visit www.ghosthunt.co.uk); and the Ghost Detective of York (tel. 07947 325239 or visit www.garygoldthorpe.com). Here are ten of the most interesting characters featured on their rounds.

The Brothers. Two 16th-century brothers mugged and killed a York priest; one then reported the other to the authorities and watched him hang, before himself going mad with guilt. Their ghosts walk St William's College, their lodging place close to York Minster.

The Duke of Buckingham. A notorious philanderer in the reign of Charles II, his ghost at the Cock and Bottle pub on Skeldergate is apparently only ever seen by women.

The Funeral Guest. Appears to funeral parties at All Saints Church on Pavement.

The Ghosts of the Old Starre Inn. This 17th-century pub on Stonegate is variously said to be haunted by soldiers, cats and an old lady.

The Grey Lady. York's most theatrical ghost – a medieval nun who was bricked up in a room of what is now the Theatre Royal after having an affair with a York nobleman.

The Headless Earl. The body of the Earl of Northumberland, executed in York for treason in 1572, wanders near Goodramgate in search of his head.

The Lady of the Golden Fleece. Lady Alice Peckett, wife of a former mayor of York and owner of the Golden Fleece, is just one of several ghosts claimed by this pub, one of the oldest in the city.

The Legionnaires. An army of Roman soldiers who walk through the walls of the Treasurer's House near the Minster.

Mad Alice. A woman hanged in 1825 haunts Lund's Court between Swinegate and Low Petergate.

The Tudor Lady. Wanders around King's Manor. The ghost is thought to be Catherine Howard, Henry VIII's fourth wife, who was executed soon after a stay here.

YORKSHIRE POEMS

'Speak of the North' by CHARLOTTE BRONTË

Speak of the North! A lonely moor
Silent and dark and trackless swells,
The waves of some wild streamlet pour
Hurriedly through its ferny dells.

Profoundly still the twilight air,
Lifeless the landscape; so we deem,
Till like a phantom gliding near
A stag bends down to drink the stream.

And far away a mountain zone,
A cold, white waste of snow-drifts lies,
And one star, large and soft and lone,
Silently lights the unclouded skies.

YORKSHIRE'S STEAM RAILWAYS

Many of the railway lines that once served Yorkshire's people and industries have fallen out of use, but the enthusiasm of volunteers has maintained several routes, running through some of the loveliest parts of the county. These seven lines are all run by preservation societies, and their lovingly restored steam locomotives provide great days out, for families and rail buffs in particular.

Derwent Valley Light Railway. Runs steam trains up and down a ½ mile (800 m) section of the original Derwent Valley Railway from the Yorkshire Museum of Farming at Murton Park. Trains run on Sundays and Bank Holidays from Easter to September. Tel. 01904 489966 or visit www.dvlr.org.uk.

The Elsecar Railway. Steam trains run for a mile (1.6 km) along this former colliery branch line of the South Yorkshire Railway between Rockingham and Hemingfield, though there are plans to extend it by another mile. Services run most Sundays from March to October, and some Saturdays during holiday times. Tel. 01226 746746 or visit www.elsecarrailway.co.nr.

Embsay and Bolton Abbey Steam Railway. Winds for 4½ miles (7.2 km) through pretty Yorkshire Dales scenery. Steam trains run every Sunday, and more frequently in the summer, on the old Skipton to Ilkley branch line after it was reclaimed by the Yorkshire Dales Railway Museum Trust. Tel. 01756 710614 or visit www.embsayboltonabbeyrailway.org.uk.

Keighley and Worth Valley Railway. Steam trains run every weekend and every day in summer along this 5 mile (8 km) line through Brontë country, from Keighley to Oxenhope via Haworth, Oakworth, Damems and Ingrow. Famous as the location of *The Railway Children* film. The line carries locals as well as tourists and offers a wonderful glimpse of the golden age of British rail. Tel. 01535 645214 or visit www.kwvr.co.uk.

Kirklees Light Railway. Little narrow gauge line with steam-pulled trains, running for 4 miles (6.4 km) through west Yorkshire. There's a visitor centre at one end of the line, in Clayton West, and picnic and play areas at the other, in Shelley. Tel. 01484 865727 or visit www.kirkleeslightrailway.com.

The Middleton Railway. Claims to be the oldest working railway in the world, having been launched by an act of parliament in 1758. It was taken over by volunteers in 1960. The journey along the mile (1.6 km) of track just south of Leeds from Moor Road to Park Halt and back takes about 25 minutes. Tel. 0113 271 0320 or visit www.middletonrailway.org.uk.

North Yorkshire Moors Railway. Magnificent 18 mile (29 km) line through the North York Moors National Park, from Pickering to Whitby. Reclaimed from a line closed by the Beeching Report and managed by a hardworking preservation trust. The second longest heritage railway in the country and almost certainly the busiest, with around 300,000 passengers a year. Steam trains run up to every hour in the summer, with a reduced timetable in winter. Stations along the way have featured in numerous films and TV series, including Goathland in ITV's *Heartbeat*. Tel. 01751 472508 or visit www.nymr.co.uk.

Steam services also run from time to time on the Settle to Carlisle railway, usually regarded as the country's most scenic railway. Visit www.settle-carlisle.co.uk for timetables.

YORKSHIRE DAY

Yorkshire Day was the brainchild of the Yorkshire Ridings Society, a group set up in 1974 to campaign for Yorkshire's territory to be recognised as the historic North, East and West Ridings and the City of York.

A day set aside for celebrating all that is special about Yorkshire seemed to the society to be a good way of advancing its aim of protecting the county's individuality and character. Its members chose 1 August – the day when Yorkshire soldiers who had fought in the Battle of Minden in Germany picked white roses as tributes to their dead comrades. Coincidentally or not, it is also the day on which slavery was officially abolished, following campaigning by Yorkshireman William Wilberforce.

Since Yorkshire Day was first organized in 1975, the event has grown in popularity and is now celebrated in most towns and villages that consider themselves part of 'real' Yorkshire. People wear white roses, take part in traditional Yorkshire games and eat local food, while mayors and other civic heads convene in one place in a gathering organised by the Yorkshire Society. Leeds, Bradford, Penistone, Hull and Redcar have been the last five hosts of meetings to 2008. Critics say the day only reinforces outdated stereotypes about Yorkshire, but supporters argue that it gives residents the chance to celebrate their heritage and preserves the 'pure' Yorkshire identity. In recent years the day has also been used to advance Yorkshire's case for its own regional government, and there have been calls for it to be designated as a public holiday.

HOW TO BUILD A DRY STONE WALL

Wherever you go in rural Yorkshire, you will never be far from a dry stone wall. Winding across the landscape, they're as distinctive a part of the Yorkshire countryside as the hills, dales and sheep.

Yorkshire has more miles of walls than anywhere else in Britain, and their sturdiness is testament to the dedicated craft and backbreaking labour of the men who built them. Though many are much older, most of Yorkshire's dry stone walls date to the 18th or 19th centuries, when they were put up to mark the boundaries of common land and to keep livestock either in or out. As the name suggests, they are walls that are built without any mortar or cement, but instead held up by the weight of each carefully laid stone. A properly laid wall is actually much sturdier than any cemented wall or wooden fence, and a good deal more attractive too. With a bit of care, dry stone walls can last centuries, withstanding the rain, snow and winds of the open countryside with ease.

But behind every yard of wall is hours of hard work, often done in dreadful weather and, on the exposed hillsides, howling gales. Building up a wall is like fitting together a very heavy and three-dimensional jigsaw puzzle, each piece an essential part of the strength and appearance of the whole. Even the most experienced builder will manage no more than a few yards of wall in a single day.

Not all stone is suitable for building, and carefully selecting materials is the waller's first job. Since a tonne or more is required for every yard of wall, getting the stone up the hillside is often the toughest job of all. After that, while a few masonry tools and supporting props are used, dry stone walls are essentially handmade. Techniques vary, but most wallers begin by digging out a small trench a few feet wide and a few inches deep, before placing large 'footing' stones snugly inside. Rows of large, flat stones are laid on top, with 'hearting' – smaller chock stones or gravel – tightly filling any gaps that remain in between. For greater strength, walls are often built in double rows parallel to each other, with occasional 'through' stones spanning both to bind them together.

The wall rises layer by layer, with each stone resting on at least two others below it. Stones must fit together tightly, so that each supports the other and gives the wall strength. For balance, the width tapers as the wall rises, becoming about an inch narrower for each foot it climbs. At the top – usually 4–5 feet (1.2-1.5 m) high – a row of 'coping' stones is sometimes laid perpendicular or flat, giving the wall a distinctive appearance. But there's a practical side too, since the spiky top makes it more difficult for sheep to clamber over.

The appearance of dry stone walls can vary quite substantially, according to the waller's style or the type of stone available in a particular area. Many have become important wildlife habitats, home to birds, insects and plants, and they often incorporate holes to allow small animals to pass through, as well as stiles for walkers to pass over. In winter, walls can also provide valuable shelter for sheep, which gather against them for protection against howling winds or snowdrifts.

The art of dry stone walling has declined over the centuries – landowners find it much cheaper and quicker to install wooden or electric fences – and many walls are now in poor condition. When it last surveyed England's stock of walls, the Countryside Agency found that nearly half were either derelict or likely to become so, a third more showed signs of deterioration, and only 4 per cent were in pristine condition. Without major conservation work, many miles of walls in Yorkshire and elsewhere are likely to fall into ruin over the coming decades.

Agencies including the National Trust and the Dry Stone Walling Association are working hard to maintain stretches of walls, and skilled wallers remain very much in demand. Dry stone walls have become rather fashionable lately, as garden features and even art installations. And in between projects, wallers can compete in the 'Grand Prix' of walling competitions run by the Dry Stone Walling Association across the country, in which they are judged on the appearance and sturdiness of a wall and the speed with which it is prepared. Several Yorkshire shows and fairs also incorporate competitions, for novices as well as experts.

YORKSHIRE SAYINGS

'Never ask a man if he's from Yorkshire. If he is, he'll tell you anyway – and if he's not, you'll only embarrass him.'

THE YORKSHIRE DALES AND THEIR MEANINGS

The Yorkshire Dales get their name from the Old Norse word *dalr*, meaning valley, and many of them – though not all – get their specific titles from their accompanying rivers. Here are the meanings of some major dales.

Airedale – the valley of the River Aire
Arkengarthdale – the valley where Arkle had his enclosure; Arkle was a Viking name and *garth* means enclosure
Bishopdale – the valley of Biscop or a similar Old English name
Coverdale – the valley of the River Cover
Deepdale – the deep valley
Dentdale – the valley of the River Dent
Garsdale – the valley of Garth, a Viking name
Langstrothdale – the valley with long marshes
Littondale – the valley with a farm on a hill, taking its name from the village of Litton
Malhamdale – the valley by the coves
Nidderdale – the valley of the River Nidd
Ribblesdale – the valley of the River Ribble
Swaledale – the valley of the River Swale
Uredale – the valley of the River Ure
Wensleydale – the valley with the clearing belonging to Waendel or similar, taking its name from the village of Wensley
Wharfedale – the valley of the River Wharfe

FAMOUS YORKSHIRE FOLK – GUY FAWKES

Along with Robin Hood, who is sometimes claimed by Yorkshire as one of its own, Guy Fawkes is the county's most famous villain, with a lasting impact on British history and culture.

Fawkes was born in 1570 in York, where he was also raised. He was baptised at the Church of St Michael le Belfrey near York Minster and educated at the still-standing St Peter's School. His father, a proctor of the ecclesiastical courts, died while Fawkes was still young. His mother remarried into a Catholic family who were opponents of the Church of England, and Fawkes himself converted to Catholicism at the age of 16 and took on much of their resentment against the Church. He served for several years as a soldier, both in England and in the Netherlands, where he fought for the Catholic Spanish army against the Protestant forces. He changed his name to the Spanish Guido and was involved in the Catholics' siege of Calais in 1596. It is thought that he tried to persuade Spain to extend its Catholic influence to England, too.

When it became clear that this wasn't going to happen, Fawkes took matters into his own hands by becoming involved in the famous 1605 Gunpowder Plot to blow up King James I and the Houses of Parliament. Recruited for his military expertise, Fawkes was to have been the man to light the dozens of barrels of gunpowder that the conspirators had stored in a cellar beneath Parliament. As he prepared to detonate the explosion to coincide with the state opening of Parliament on 5 November, Fawkes was discovered, tortured and hanged the following January.

Although he wasn't the leader of the conspirators, Fawkes is forever associated with the plot, while the names of his colleagues are largely forgotten. His name lives on in the annual Bonfire Night and firework celebrations of England and elsewhere, and he has also been referenced by numerous writers, artists and singers.

YORKSHIRE'S UNIVERSITIES

The Yorkshire and Humber region is home to ten universities. They are:

University of Bradford
University of Huddersfield
University of Hull
University of Leeds
Leeds Metropolitan University
University of Sheffield
Sheffield Hallam University
University of Teesside (Middlesbrough)
University of York
York St John University

Hull is also home to a campus of the University of Lincoln, formerly Humberside University.

THE THREE PEAKS

The Three Peaks Challenge is one of England's great walks, and a fine way to see the best of the Yorkshire Dales. The trio of fells are **Pen-y-Ghent** (2,277 feet or 694 m), **Whernside** (2,415 feet or 736 m) and **Ingleborough** (2,372 feet or 723 m), and from the usual starting point of Horton-in-Ribblesdale it's a circular walk of 23 to 25 miles (37–40 km), depending on how direct you want to make it.

You can take as long as you like over the walk, of course, and it's a decent achievement just to get round. But walkers seem to like a challenge, and the usual one here is to complete the circuit in less than 12 hours. Doing so entitles you to membership of the Three Peaks of Yorkshire club, administered by the people at the Pen-y-Ghent café in

Horton. Walkers can clock out at the café by leaving their details, and clock in on their return – a useful service that ensures the mountain rescue team will come looking for you if you go astray and that provides proof of completing the challenge to anyone who doubts you. Well over 200,000 people are thought to have done the walk since the café started keeping records.

The Three Peaks circle is also the route of a popular fell-running race that has been staged annually since 1954. Anyone feeling justifiably pleased with themselves after getting round in 11 or 12 hours will be interested to hear that the men's record for completing the route is a mind-boggling 2 hours 46 minutes.

Yorkshire's Three Peaks walk is not to be confused with Britain's challenge of the same name, taking in the highest mountains in England, Scotland and Wales – Scafell Pike, Ben Nevis and Snowdon. The challenge there is to complete three climbs within 24 hours, something that requires some speedy driving as well as nimble climbing.

THE REAL HUMPTY DUMPTY AND GRAND OLD DUKE OF YORK

There have been several theories for the origins of the famous nursery rhymes about Humpty Dumpty and the Duke of York, but Yorkshire is convinced that this is the home of both.

According to locals, the real-life Humpty Dumpty is Cardinal Thomas Wolsey, who lived for some time at Cawood Castle, the Archbishop of York's residence between York and Selby. Wolsey was certainly short and somewhat egg-shaped, like Humpty Dumpty, and the wall on which he sat is reckoned to be Cawood's great tower, to which he often went to think. The great fall is Wolsey's sudden falling out with Henry VIII in 1530 over the king's plans to divorce Catherine of Aragon and marry Anne Boleyn. The nursery rhyme's line about the king's horses and men indicates the forces sent to Cawood to arrest Wolsey for treason, while the 'Couldn't put Humpty together again' line refers to the fact that Wolsey died on his way to London to face the charges.

The rhyme certainly seems to fit Yorkshire's theory, though other historians have linked Humpty Dumpty to the downfalls of several monarchs, or even to a cannon so nicknamed during the Civil War. Cawood Castle was mostly destroyed in the Civil War and its aftermath, though the gatehouse and banqueting hall remain, with parts restored by the Landmark Trust into holiday accommodation.

There are similarly several conflicting claims to the source of 'The Grand Old Duke of York'. One of the most popular links it to a Flanders campaign in the 1790s by Prince Frederick, Duke of York, which resulted in a victory then defeat – hence the marching of troops up and then down again. But Yorkshire has at least two versions of the rhyme's origins. One also involves Prince Frederick – this time during his time in charge of Allerton Castle, when he had a Temple of Victory built on a large hill in the grounds, near the modern-day A1. The sight of men going up and down the hill is said to have prompted the verse.

The second version dates it back much further, to the Wars of the Roses in 1460 when Richard, Duke of York, marched his men up to Sandal Castle before going down again to face the Lancastrians in the Battle of Wakefield. There have been some doubts about whether Richard's army was as large as the 'ten thousand men' of the rhyme, though the outcome of the battle – the death of Richard and many of his men – would seem to fit its mocking tone.

YORKSHIRE'S PLACE IN THE WORLD

The most recent figures from the Office for National Statistics estimated the population of Yorkshire and the Humber at 5,142,000. As this table shows, that makes it bigger in terms of residents than Norway and Singapore – but slightly smaller than Finland and Nicaragua. Population estimates are from *The CIA 2008 World Factbook* in the US and are based on mid-2007.

Country	Population
Nicaragua	5,675,356
Denmark	5,468,120
Kyrgyzstan	5,447,502
Slovakia	5,284,149
Finland	5,238,460
Yorkshire	**5,142,000**
Turkmenistan	5,097,028
Eritrea	4,906,585
Georgia	4,646,003
Norway	4,627,926
Singapore	4,553,009

The area of the Yorkshire and Humber region is 5,950 square miles (15,413 sq km). That puts it in the odd company of Swaziland and Timor-Leste in size terms. Country estimates are again from *The CIA 2008 World Factbook*.

Country	Area in sq miles (sq km)
Slovenia	7,825 (20,273)
New Caledonia	7,357 (19,060)
Fiji	7,052 (18,270)
Kuwait	6,878 (17,820)
Swaziland	6,702 (17,363)
Yorkshire	**5,950 (15,413)**
Timor-Leste	5,793 (15,007)
Montenegro	5,414 (14,026)
The Bahamas	5,380 (13,940)
Puerto Rico	5,323 (13,790)

YORKSHIRE INDUSTRY – STEEL

While west Yorkshire built a reputation for textiles, the south developed heavier industries – and in Sheffield's case steel.

Once the biggest producer in the world, Sheffield and steel remain inextricably tied, even though the industry's workforce is now a fraction of what it once was. And while the Industrial Revolution was the making of it, the city's reputation for steel stretches much further back. There is evidence of the manufacture of cutlery, axes and other metal items at least as long ago as the 14th century – Geoffrey Chaucer mentions a man carrying a Sheffield knife – and by the 17th century up to half of all men in the city were working as cutlers. Sheffield and its surroundings had all the resources needed for heavy industry of this sort: rich supplies of iron and coal from the hillsides, water from the rivers for power and wood and charcoal from the forests to burn.

Into the 18th century the local steel masters began to build their own cementation furnaces and, then, to master the 'melting pot' process of crucible steel. By Victorian times there were several hundred furnaces in Sheffield, and the city was the world's leading steel exporter with a reputation for high quality as well as quantity. The thriving industry rapidly expanded Sheffield's population and brought in fortunes for the furnace and factory bosses. But conditions for the workforce were unpleasant and often hugely dangerous, matched only by the squalid, desperately overcrowded terraces in which most of them lived. Growing resentment led to the rise of trade unions, and the city soon had a reputation for its militant workforce.

Sheffield's industry was further transformed by the development of stainless steel by Harry Brearley, a steel researcher born in the city. Investigating the problems of erosion on gun barrels, he altered levels of chromium in the steel mix to achieve what he called 'rustless steel', resistant to rust and markings. His discovery wasn't universally acclaimed – one critic called his product 'the knife that would not cut' – but the benefits of rust-free cutlery soon became obvious and the name 'stainless steel' was coined.

Sheffield was an obvious centre for arms manufacture during the two world wars – and consequently an equally obvious target for German bombing. Changing markets, new technologies and cheap imports hit the steel industry hard after the Second World War, forcing many firms to close or merge. But although jobs have been shed over the years since, Sheffield now produces more steel than ever, in a cleaner, safer and much less labour-intensive way than in the past. The Sheffield Industrial Museums Trust looks after several of the city's old steel and iron sites, among them the Kelham Island and Shepherd Wheel Museums and the Abbeydale Industrial Hamlet.

⊛ ⊛ ⊛ ⊛ ⊛ ⊛ ⊛ ⊛ ⊛ ⊛ ⊛

BETTY'S STORY

Bettys Tea Rooms is a Yorkshire institution and the number one place for afternoon tea and cakes for any visitor. But like many English traditions, it was actually founded by an immigrant – Swiss confectioner Frederick Belmont. Belmont came to England to start his own business, and legend has it that he took a wrong train when he arrived in London, eventually finding himself not on the south coast as he had intended but somewhere in Yorkshire. Fortunately he soon got over the shock, and finding that the countryside reminded him of home he settled in the county. He opened Bettys in Harrogate in 1919, and his Swiss cakes and teas found instant popularity in the genteel spa town. Belmont soon added a bakery and a second tea rooms in York, which remains the flagship branch of the chain.

Bettys has flourished pretty much ever since, its combination of traditionally elegant surroundings, fancy cakes and down-to-earth Yorkshire hospitality making it a particular hit with tourists. It now has branches in Ilkley, Northallerton and the RHS Gardens at Harlow Carr as well as Harrogate and York, plus a mail order business and a cookery school. In the 1960s it joined forces with tea and coffee merchants Taylors, whose lines include the popular Yorkshire Tea. But despite queues out of the tea rooms' doors at most times, and plenty of opportunities to grow the Bettys brand, the company has so far resisted the temptation to extend beyond Yorkshire. It remains a family-owned business, based where it all began in Harrogate.

For some reason the story of how Bettys got its name was never passed on by Belmont – or else the company is keeping it a very good secret – and her identity remains a mystery. One theory goes that Betty was the Queen Mother – Elizabeth Bowes Lyons – who would have been in her late teens when the first shop opened. Another has it that the inspiration was Betty Lupton, the well-known manageress of Harrogate Spa – or else a small girl who had died of tuberculosis on the site of the first branch. And another story relates that another girl called Betty had interrupted a meeting called by Belmont to discuss the shop's name – and in doing so solved the problem.

ENGLAND'S LONGEST PLACE-NAME

With 27 letters and a couple of hyphens for good measure, the longest single word place-name in Yorkshire – and England, too – is Sutton-under-Whitestonecliffe. The village is located a few miles east of the much more succinctly named Thirsk. But it's still dwarfed by Britain's longest place-name – Llanfairpwllgwyngyllgogerychwyrndrobwllllantysiliogogogoch – on the island of Anglesey.

CURIOSITIES AT THE WHITBY MUSEUM

Whitby Museum was opened in the 1820s by the Whitby Literary and Philosophical Society with the aim of educating the town's people. Since then it has gathered a startling array of exhibits, many of them relating to Whitby's interesting history but some of them seemingly relating to very little at all. Here are ten of the thousands of items on display at this wonderfully old-fashioned and entertaining museum.

The Tempest Prognosticator, a barometer worked by
12 bottled leeches

The Hand of Glory, a hand cut from a dead body on a
gibbet and baked hard, used as a talisman

Victorian false teeth

Weeping willow from the tomb of Napoleon

A witchpost, used to ward off witches on the North York Moors

Totem pole from the Nootka Sound in the Pacific Ocean

Clog and ankle chain worn by school truants

A model ship in a light bulb

Full suit of Japanese samurai warrior armour

Miniature Noah's Ark made by French prisoners of war

YORKSHIRE'S MPS

If Yorkshire had a political map it would be overwhelmingly red. Of the 56 seats in the House of Commons returned by the Yorkshire and Humber region, 44 are held by Labour MPs, nine by Conservatives and three by Liberal Democrats. Well-known Yorkshire MPs include John Prescott, David Blunkett, Ed Balls, William Hague and Nick Clegg.

Yorkshire's constituencies and the MPs elected to serve them in the 2005 General Election are:

Barnsley Central - Eric Illsley, Labour
Barnsley East and Mexborough - Jeff Ennis, Labour
Barnsley West and Penistone - Michael Clapham, Labour
Batley and Spen - Mike Wood, Labour
Beverley and Holderness - Graham Stuart, Conservative
Bradford North - Terry Rooney, Labour
Bradford South - Gerry Sutcliffe, Labour
Bradford West - Marsha Singh, Labour
Brigg and Goole - Ian Cawsey, Labour
Calder Valley - Christine McAfferty, Labour
City of York - Hugh Bayley, Labour
Cleethorpes - Shona McIsaac, Labour
Colne Valley - Kali Mountford, Labour
Dewsbury - Shahid Malik, Labour
Don Valley - Caroline Flint, Labour
Doncaster Central - Rosie Winterton, Labour
Doncaster North - Ed Miliband, Labour
Elmet - Colin Burgon, Labour
Great Grimsby - Austin Mitchell, Labour
Halifax - Linda Riordan, Labour
Haltemprice and Howden - David Davis, Conservative
Harrogate and Knaresborough- Phil Willis, Liberal Democrat
Hemsworth - Jon Trickett, Labour
Huddersfield - Barry Sheerman, Labour
Hull East - John Prescott, Labour
Hull North - Diana Johnson, Labour
Hull West and Hessle - Alan Johnson, Labour

Keighley and Ilkley – Ann Cryer, Labour
Leeds Central – Hilary Benn, Labour
Leeds East – George Mudie, Labour
Leeds North East – Fabian Hamilton, Labour
Leeds North West – Greg Mulholland, Liberal Democrat
Leeds West – John Battle, Labour
Morley and Rothwell – Colin Challen, Labour
Normanton – Ed Balls, Labour
Pontefract and Castleford – Yvette Cooper, Labour
Pudsey – Paul Truswell, Labour
Richmond – William Hague, Conservative
Rother Valley – Kevin Barron, Labour
Rotherham – Denis McShane, Labour
Ryedale – John Greenway, Conservative
Scarborough and Whitby – Robert Goodwill, Conservative
Scunthorpe – Elliot Morley, Labour
Selby – John Grogan, Labour
Sheffield Attercliffe – Clive Betts, Labour
Sheffield Brightside – David Blunkett, Labour
Sheffield Central – Richard Caborn, Labour
Sheffield Hallam – Nick Clegg, Liberal Democrat
Sheffield Heeley – Meg Munn, Labour
Sheffield Hillsborough – Angela Smith, Labour
Shipley – Philip Davies, Conservative
Skipton and Ripon – David Curry, Conservative
Vale of York – Anne McIntosh, Conservative
Wakefield – Mary Creagh, Labour
Wentworth – John Healey, Labour
Yorkshire East – Greg Knight, Conservative

THE FOUR CORNERS OF YORKSHIRE

The most northerly, southerly, easterly and westerly inhabited places of Yorkshire – defined here as the three Ridings prior to the reorganisation of boundaries in 1974.

Northerly – **Holwick**, near Middleton-in-Teesdale; now part of County Durham for administrative purposes

Southerly – **Netherthorpe**, southeast of Sheffield; now part of Derbyshire

Easterly – **Kilnsea** on Spurn Head; now part of the
East Riding of Yorkshire

Westerly – **Low Bentham**, now part of North Yorkshire

EMMERDALE'S DISASTERS

Emmerdale is undoubtedly Yorkshire's most violent village and quite possibly one of the most dangerous places in the world in which to live. Since the soap began in 1972 dozens of residents have been murdered or killed in dreadful accidents, and the fictional village has suffered numerous major disasters, including a plane crash and ferocious storm.

Emmerdale seems to have become particularly accident-prone over the last few years. As this list of some of the most noteworthy incidents shows, the village particularly needs major improvements to its road safety, serious education about the dangers of fire and a few more policemen on the streets.

1987   Jackie Merrick falls down a mineshaft
1988   The Post Office is targeted in an armed robbery
1990   A chemical tanker crashes into a wall
1993   A plane crash wrecks the village
          A farm collapses from subsidence
1994   There is another armed robbery at the Post Office
1995   A car crashes into a tree and explodes, killing Luke McAllister
1996   A fire after a wedding kills Dave Glover
1997   A cocaine-fuelled car smash kills Linda Fowler
1998   There is a third armed robbery at the Post Office
1999   Rachel Hughes is killed after her boyfriend pushes her
          off a cliff
2000   A collision between a van and minibus kills Pete Collins
          and Butch Dingle
          A barn fire kills Sarah Sugden
2001   A speeding stolen car kills Jean Strickland
2002   The church is burned down
          A car crash kills Angie Reynolds
2003   An apocalyptic storm wrecks the village and kills
          Tricia Dingle
2005   Shelley Williams is pushed off a boat and drowns
          Home Farm is destroyed in a deliberately caused gas explosion
          A car crashes into a brick wall and explodes, killing Max King

2006 An explosion in a show home kills three people
The vicarage is burned down
Tom King is killed on Christmas Day after his son pushes him
out of a window

2007 Policewoman Grace Barraclough is killed after being run over
by a lorry
Billy Hopwood is trapped in a fire that causes aerosols to
explode

WHO OWNS THE NATIONAL PARKS?

The land on the three National Parks wholly or partly within Yorkshire
is mostly privately owned, though the easing of access rights means
much of it is now accessible to walkers. The Forestry Commission is a
significant landowner on the North York Moors, while the National
Trust, local water boards and the Ministry of Defence each have patches
of land under their control.

	Yorkshire Dales	North York Moors	Peak District
Private ownership	95.0%	79.9%	62.0%
Forestry Commission	—	16.6%	—
National Trust	3.5%	1.2%	12.2%
Natural England	0.7%	—	—
Yorkshire Water	0.3%	0.1%	3.3%
North West Water	—	—	7.1%
Severn Trent Water	—	—	1.3%
Ministry of Defence	0.3%	0.5%	—
National Park Authority	0.1%	0.6%	4.8%
Yorkshire Wildlife Trust	0.1%	—	—
Chatsworth	—	—	3.0%
Sheffield City Council	—	—	2.1%
Other	—	1.1%	4.2%

THE SOURCE OF YORKSHIRE'S TOURISTS

The most common countries of origin of overseas visitors to Yorkshire
are the USA and Germany, according to data from the Yorkshire Tourist
Board. Here's the full breakdown of visitors from abroad in 2006.

Country of origin	Percentage of total trips made by overseas residents
USA	.11
Germany	.11
Spain	.9
France	.8
The Netherlands	.5
Ireland	.5
Australia	.5
Canada	.4
Norway	.3
Italy	.3
Belgium	.3
Other	.33

YORKS AROUND THE WORLD

As Britain's global influence spread, Yorkshire's historic capital city of York inspired dozens of similarly named places around the world. Here are ten of the most interesting.

Cape York, Greenland. An isolated wilderness in northwest Greenland, discovered by English polar explorers in the 19th century.

Cape York, Queensland, Australia. A wild, inaccessible area on the rugged northern coast of Australia - possibly the furthest of all Yorks from Yorkshire's version in both distance and character.

New York, New York, USA. The most famous of York's descendants. The city and state were both named for its proprietor, James, Duke of York, after the British took the area in the 17th century.

York, Alabama, USA. Small town of 3,000 people in the heart of the civil rights movement country.

York, Maine, USA. A fishing village that became a sizeable tourist destination.

York, Nebraska, USA. Remote Midwest town of 8,000 people, founded in the 1870s and probably named after the English York rather than any of the American ones.

York, North Dakota, USA. Named by settlers - along with nearby Leeds and Rugby - after its English counterpart. Once a major rail town, now home to only a handful of people.

York, Pennsylvania, USA. Claims to be the capital of the fledgling United States and the place where the first constitution was drafted.

York, Western Australia. Settled by English explorers in the 1830s, and sprang into life during the gold rush of the 1890s.

York County, Canada. A sizeable region of north Canada, like New York named after its commander, the Duke of York. The city of Toronto was also known as York in the early 19th century.

THE YORKSHIRE DECLARATION OF INTEGRITY

As read by all true Yorkshiremen and women on Yorkshire Day, 1 August.

'I, [name], being a resident of the [West/North/East] Riding of Yorkshire [or City of York] declare:

That Yorkshire is three Ridings and the City of York, with these boundaries of 1,133 years standing;

That the address of all places in these Ridings is Yorkshire;

That all persons born therein or resident therein and loyal to the Ridings are Yorkshire men and women;

That any person or corporate body which deliberately ignores or denies the aforementioned shall forfeit all claim to Yorkshire status.

These declarations made this Yorkshire Day, [year]. God Save the Queen!'

The declaration was written by the Yorkshire Ridings Society as part of its campaign to recognize Yorkshire's historic borders and ignore the new administrative boundaries devised by the government in 1974. It is read across Yorkshire, but especially in York - the city where the historic three Ridings meet. It is often read in various dialects to remember Yorkshire's history and heritage.

YORKSHIRE FOOD – LIQUORICE

Of all the foods produced in Yorkshire, liquorice is the one that raises the most eyebrows when the identity of its source is revealed.

How Pontefract in west Yorkshire came to be such a centre for the sweet black stuff is something of a mystery, though it may have been brought over by either the Romans, crusaders or Benedictine monks from its native - and rather warmer - climates like southern Europe or Asia. No matter how it arrived, Pontefract and liquorice were being associated by the 16th century, the deep, soft, rich soil of the area having been found to be ideal for cultivating the root. Records show that there were dozens of growers by the middle of the 18th century, and entire families would be involved in collecting the harvest each year.

Liquorice root has been used for medicinal purposes since ancient times, but Pontefract pioneered its use in sweets and other edibles by boiling the root and evaporating the water to collect the extract. Adding in sugar produced a recipe for Pontefract liquorice cakes, made by softening and forming small pieces of the extract into lozenges, each stamped with the maker's symbol. The whole process was done by hand, usually by women of the town who each turned out thousands of sweets a day. Otherwise known as cakers, thumpers or - after the old name for the town - Pomfret cakes, they became a popular sweet across the country, sealing Pontefract's close associations with liquorice.

After industrialisation, what was once a cottage industry moved into factories, and by the 1920s there were around a dozen in the town, producing hundreds of tonnes a week for export all over the world. But falling demand and the rising costs associated with cultivating the root - which takes several years - gradually whittled down the industry. The last liquorice fields had gone by the middle of the 20th century, and the couple of factories now left in the town, both owned by multinational confectionery giants, import their root. In an attempt to revive the liquorice links, the Pontefract Liquorice Trust has been set up to help honour the town's sweet history. It organises a family-centred festival and Liquorice Day each July, showcasing a vast array of intriguing liquorice-flavoured products, including beer, sausages, pies and cheese as well as sweets.

FAMOUS YORKSHIRE FOLK - ALAN BENNETT

Although his work has gathered acclaim all over the world, Alan Bennett is still intimately associated with his Yorkshire roots.

Born in Leeds in 1934, Bennett first became known for his work with Peter Cook, Dudley Moore and Jonathan Miller in the satirical *Beyond the Fringe*. A prolific and very versatile writer, he has produced work for film, TV, radio, stage and books, his best known pieces including *Talking Heads*, a series of monologues for TV, and *The History Boys* and *The Madness of George III*, both successful plays turned into successful films. Unusually, he has received critical acclaim in every genre in which he has written, and his reputation has grown consistently over the years. Though his output has slowed lately, his recent autobiographical pieces for TV and page, *Telling Tales* and *Untold Stories*, have been hugely popular. He is now regarded as among the best British TV and film screenplay writers of modern times, and his reputations as a stage playwright and story writer are not far behind. He has won a host of awards, but has turned down honours, including a knighthood.

Bennett's writing has always been wrapped up in distinctively northern dialect and emotion, and much of it harks back to the places, preoccupations and eccentricities of his Yorkshire upbringing. It is sometimes difficult to work out the line between autobiography and imagination, but many of his characters, ordinary and extraordinary at the same time, are clearly the result of his uncanny observational eye and ear. Bennett's work has often been enhanced by reading in his own expressive Yorkshire voice, which has also been used to good effect on a narration of A.A. Milne's Winnie the Pooh stories. There has probably been no better chronicler of Yorkshire wit and English reserve, and though this has sometimes led to him being pigeonholed as a writer of limited range and appeal, his work has always been much more rich, incisive and compassionate than he is often given credit for.

THE VAMPIRE TOWN

Yorkshire's coastal town of Whitby has plenty of attractions for visitors, but one of its biggest draws is its connection with Bram Stoker's masterpiece of horror and suspense - *Dracula*.

The pretty, genteel town might seem to be an odd source of inspiration for one of the most terrifying novels of all time, but its distinctive landscape struck an instant chord with Stoker. While staying in Whitby, the writer went to the local library to research the vampire novel he had been working on, learning more about eastern European legends and discovering that Dracula was the Wallachian word for devil. Struck by the air of Gothic menace about the town, he decided to incorporate it into his book and to set several key scenes there.

Stoker had been particularly taken by Whitby's Catholic abbey, originally built around 637 but later redone in the Gothic style and by now in atmospheric ruins on the cliffs above the town. The view across the harbour to the abbey and the nearby church fuelled his imagination and became the setting for the shipwreck that brings Count Dracula to England. Stoker had heard from locals about a wreck that had washed dozens of coffins and dead bodies ashore, and he adapted the story for the means of bringing Dracula to Whitby via the Russian ship *Demeter*, in the form of a huge black dog. The stone steps up to the abbey are the ones up which Dracula bounds from the wreck.

Stoker incorporated into *Dracula* plenty of other sights and sounds, both around Whitby and in the Royal Hotel where he stayed. The view that inspired him is now marked by the Bram Stoker Memorial Seat on the west cliff. Along with the abbey, it is a point of pilgrimage for plenty of tourists, many of them dressed all in black in the Gothic style. Though Stoker's novel was not an instant hit, the dozens of film, TV and stage adaptations since his death in 1912 have ensured a steady flow of *Dracula* fans and a sizeable, if sinister, tourist industry.

ENGLAND'S HIGHEST PUB

Yorkshire is home to the highest public house in England – the Tan Hill Inn. Near the join of Swaledale and Arkengarthdale in the Yorkshire Dales, it sits at 1,730 feet (530 m) above sea level and ambitiously promotes itself as 'At the Top of the World'. The pub was built in 1737 to serve local miners and packhorse traders on their way over the Pennines, and the modern-day Pennine Way runs right by. The Tan Hill Inn's other claim to fame is that it became the first pub in Britain to secure a licence to host marriages when restrictions were eased in the mid-1990s. The second and third highest pubs in England are the Cat and Fiddle Inn in Cheshire (1,690 feet or 515 m) and the Kirkstone Pass Inn in Cumbria (1,480 feet or 450 m).

THE ETYMOLOGY OF SOME YORKSHIRE PLACE-NAMES

Many of the towns and cities of Yorkshire have seen subtle changes in their names over the centuries. Most of the alterations give clues to who was in charge of them at the time, and their frequency shows how often control has changed hands. Here are the changing names of six Yorkshire places; names marked with an asterisk are as recorded in the Domesday Book of 1086.

Bretlinton* • Bridelinto • Breddelington • Briddelington •
Bridlington

Cataractone • Cataractam Uicium • Catrice* • Cateriz • Kateriz •
Catrich • Catrik • Catteryke • Catheryk • **Catterick**

Oderesfelt* • Hudresfeld • Huddersfeld • **Huddersfield**

Humbrae Fluminis • Burgus super Humbre • Kengeston-on-Hulle •
Villa Regia super Hull • Kengstown super Hull • **Kingston-upon-Hull**

Mechesburg* • Mekesburc • Mikesburg • Mexseburgh • **Mexbrough**

Eboracum • Eoferwicceastre • Eoforwic • Everwic • Euruic* •
Eoforwic • Ewerwic • Jorc • Yhorke • Yorke • **York**

THE YORKSHIRE GAME OF QUOITS

As it does for many things, Yorkshire claims to be the home, in Britain at least, of the sport of quoits. While there is no firm evidence to show it was played here before anywhere else, Yorkshire is probably the country's headquarters of the game and the place where its modern history begins.

Quoits essentially involves throwing a metal ring over a post made of iron or wood, but there is much more to the game than meets the eye. It needs strength as well as skill, since the rings can be heavy and must be thrown 30–65 feet (10–20 m). The post is usually fixed in a patch of clay, helping to keep quoits in place once they have landed.

The sport began using horseshoes and dates back centuries, perhaps as far as the first Greek Olympiad, when it may have been played as a variation of discus throwing. It was popular in England by the second millennium, and became particularly popular in mining communities, who would make the rings from leftover metals. By the 15th century it was a well-organised sport, its working-class preserve and connections with pubs giving it a reputation as something of an unruly activity. In the 1880s quoits clubs and players in Yorkshire and elsewhere in the north got together to lay out the rules of 'The Northern Game'. Like some other sports, including rugby, disagreements over the rules have led to various versions of the game being devised elsewhere in the country, using different scoring systems, heavier or lighter rings and longer or shorter throwing distances.

Though it has lost much of its popularity, quoits clubs and leagues can still be found, many of them still attached to pubs, and competitions can be seen at country shows across Yorkshire, especially in the Dales. Having been exported by settlers, the game is also popular in pockets of the US.

Quoits lingo

Hob - the pin over which quoits must land

Ringer - a quoit that has landed on the hob

Gater - a quoit that lands with its edge against the hob

Hill - the top surface of the quoit

Hole - the bottom surface of the quoit

Bibber - the thrower's helper or coach

Front, **side** or **back toucher** - a quoit that lands touching
the side of the hob

YORKSHIRE'S LARGEST LAKES

The largest natural, freshwater lake in Yorkshire is Hornsea Mere, about a mile inland from the North Sea at Hornsea. At its longest point the lake is 2 miles (3 km) from top to bottom, and about ¾ mile (1 km) across at its widest point. Its total surface area is 467 acres (1.9 sq km or 0.7 sq miles). The lake is popular with watersports enthusiasts, including sailors and rowers, and is also an important spot for birdwatching.

The biggest natural lake in the Dales is Semerwater, stretching nearly ½ mile (800 m) from top to bottom and about ¼ mile (400 m) across. It's popular for sailing and canoeing as well as fishing, and plenty of Yorkshire Dales walks pass close by. Like many notable landmarks in Yorkshire, it has a local legend attached to it - in this case that a large and prosperous community once lived where the lake now is. It was visited one night by an old man begging hospitality from door to door, but he was turned down by everyone except for a shepherd and his wife. When he woke the next morning, he put a curse on the entire town apart from the place where he had stayed, perched higher than the other houses on a hillside. The waters immediately rose and drowned the town of Semer. The story has inspired several poems, though none of them can explain where the lost city fits in a lake that is only a few feet deep in most places.

Elsewhere in the Dales, Malham Tarn is slightly bigger than Semerwater in surface area, but owes much of its size to artificial enlargement. In

1791 the tarn was raised by about 3 feet (1 m), flooding the previous shoreline. The tarn has rich stocks of trout and a bird sanctuary on its western side is part of a nature reserve. Other sizeable tarns in the Dales, from a total of around a hundred, include Birkdale Tarn in Upper Swaledale and Birks Tarn on Birks Fell.

THE BATTLE OF THE BEERS

The Black Sheep Brewery at Masham in north Yorkshire is now one of the successful beer makers in the county, but its beginnings were distinctly acrimonious.

Until the early 1990s Masham was dominated by one brewery: Theakstons. After 160 years of family ownership – the last few of them marred by wrangling among family members – the independent company was bought in 1987 by the giant Scottish & Newcastle Breweries. It was the latest of several such firms to fall into new hands, causing despair among real ale aficionados and also alienating Paul Theakston, a member of the brewing family but firmly opposed to the corporate intervention.

Determined to continue brewing as an independent, he decided to tackle Theakstons' new owners on their own patch. He bought a derelict old brewing plant in Masham and snapped up equipment from other breweries closing down in the Lake District and Nottingham as well as elsewhere in Yorkshire, using it to return to traditional techniques of brewing. He wanted to use the name of the old brewing plant, Lightfoot's, but found that Theakstons had registered it. So, in a nod to his falling out with the rest of the family – as well as to Masham's farming heritage and the residents of its fields – he called it the Black Sheep Brewery.

The new plant produced its first beers in 1992 and has since picked up plenty of awards and acclaim. It now produces tens of thousands of barrels a year from its newly expanded site and also hosts a popular visitors' centre. It has added to its different beers with brews named after Yorkshire's TV soap *Emmerdale* and Riggwelter, which takes its name from Yorkshire dialect for a sheep stuck on its back and unable to get up – much like excessive Black Sheep drinkers. Careful nurturing of the brewery's brand and a revival of support for small breweries over the multinationals means Black Sheep is now as widely known as the Theakston name that begot it.

NATIONAL TRUST PROPERTIES IN YORKSHIRE

The National Trust has taken care of sizeable chunks of Yorkshire and several of its grand homes since it was founded in 1895. The 21 National Trust properties and areas of land open to the public are:

Beningborough Hall, York. An 18th-century mansion stuffed with portraits, with expansive gardens.

Braithwaite Hall, East Witton. A large 17th-century farm, still working under tenancy from the National Trust.

Bridestones, Crosscliff and Blakey Topping. Some 1,200 acres (485 ha) of moorland, woodland and farmland within the North York Moors National Park.

Brimham Rocks, Summerbridge. Moorland rock to a height of a thousand feet (305 m) with fine views over Nidderdale.

East Riddlesden Hall, Keighley. A 17th-century manor house with varied gardens, built by a Yorkshire cloth merchant from a rather disreputable family.

Fountains Abbey and Studley Royal Water Garden, Ripon. The atmospheric shell of a Cistercian abbey founded in 1132 and the largest monastic ruins anywhere in Britain. One of only two World Heritage Sites in Yorkshire.

Goddards Garden, York. The garden of Noel Goddard Terry of the Terry's chocolate manufacturing family. The house is the headquarters of the National Trust in Yorkshire.

Hardcastle Crags, Hebden Bridge. A woodland valley over 400 acres (162 ha), including Gibson Mill, once a cotton mill and now an energy self-sufficient visitor centre.

Maister House, Hull. The grand 18th-century house of the Maisters, one of Hull's leading merchant families during its trading heyday.

Malham Tarn Estate. There are 7,000 acres (2,830 ha) of moorland and limestone pavements in the Yorkshire Dales. The tarn is a National Nature Reserve with some rare birds, animals and plants.

Marsden Moor Estate. A moorland area around the village of Marsden in Yorkshire's slice of the Peak District. Hosts some rare wildlife and various archaeological finds.

Moulton Hall, Richmond. An Elizabethan manor house, open to the public by prior arrangement.

Mount Grace Priory, Northallerton. The ruin of a Carthusian priory from the 14th century, one of the best preserved such sites in the country.

Nostell Priory, Wakefield. A fine 18th-century house on the site of a medieval priory, with grand rooms, superb art and furniture and parkland with lakes.

Nunnington Hall, York. A manor house by the River Rye, probably originally built in the 13th century but redone in the 17th and 18th centuries.

Ormesby Hall, Middlesbrough. A Palladian mansion house owned by the Pennyman family from the 16th century up to the 1980s.

Rievaulx Terrace, Helmsley. 18th-century landscaped gardens with two temples and views of Ryedale and Rievaulx Abbey, looked after by English Heritage.

Roseberry Topping, Newton-under-Roseberry. A 1,000 foot (305 m) hill with views of the Yorkshire Dales.

Treasurer's House, York. A medieval town house close to York Minster, restored in the early 20th century. Supposedly haunted.

Upper Wharfedale. There are 6,000 acres (2,430 ha) of classic Yorkshire Dales territory, home to several National Trust farms and villages.

Yorkshire Coast, from Filey to Saltburn. A spectacular stretch of coastline, taking in Robin Hood's Bay and varied habitats.

In 2006–7 the most popular National Trust property for which admission is charged was Fountains Abbey and Studley Royal Water Garden, drawing 313,388 visitors.

A YORKSHIRE DICTIONARY

Part 2 : N to Z

More words from the Yorkshire vocabulary and their meanings for those less fluent in the Tyke tongue.

nay – no • neb – nose • nebber – flat cap • neet – night •
nessy – outside lavatory • nimm – to steal • nithered – cold •
nivver – never • nobbut – only • nooa – no • nowt – nothing •
ommost – almost • ooad – old • oss – to try •

'ow do – how are you? • owt – anything • oyl – hole •
parky – chilly • paws – hands • pined – hungry • prog – food •
puckly – cloudy • pund – pound • raffled – knotted •
rammle – to wander • ranty – wild, excited •
rawky – cold and misty • reet – right • reng – wrong •
ronce – to climb up • rovven – torn • ruiz – to drink heavily •
sam – to pick up • scary – stony • scoddy – poor • scran – food •
sewer – sure • sholl – to slip • shoot – to shout • sich or sike – such •
side – clear • sile down – rain heavily • sin – since •
sithee – goodbye • skeg – to glance • skitter – to hurry off •
sluffed – disheartened • snell – cold and wet • snig – to haul •
spak – spoke • splauder – to spread out • strang – strong •
stunt – obstinate • summat – something • sup – to drink •
ta – thanks • tahme – time • tak or tek – to take • teem – to pour •
tew – to work hard • tha or thee – you • throng – busy •
thysen or thysel – yourself • tonn – to turn • traps – belongings •
us-sen – ourselves • varra or varry – very • wad – would •
wark – work • watter – water • wekken – to wake • wer – our •
what-for – punishment • wivoot – without •
wrang or wreng – wrong • wuthering – wild winds • yam – home •
yan – one • yat – hot • yersel – yourself • yesterneet – last night •
youd – to nag

YORKSHIRE'S NOBEL PRIZE WINNERS

Yorkshire can lay claim by birth to eight winners of the Nobel Prize.
Remarkably, two of them were born around the same town, Todmorden,
and even had the same physics teacher at school; while another two
were born in Halifax. In order of receiving the Prize, Yorkshire's eight
Nobel laureates are:

Owen Willans Richardson (1879-1959; born in Dewsbury). Awarded
the Prize for Physics in 1928 for his research into thermionics.

Edward Appleton (1892-1965; born in Bradford). Awarded the Prize
for Physics in 1947 for his discovery of the ionosphere, which advanced
the use of radar.

John Cockcroft (1897-1967; born in Todmorden). Jointly awarded
the Prize for Physics in 1951 for splitting the atom and launching the
British nuclear industry.

George Porter (1920–2002; born in Stainforth). Jointly awarded the
Prize for Chemistry in 1967 for work on chemical reactions.

Geoffrey Wilkinson (1921–96; born in Springside near Todmorden). Jointly awarded the Prize for Chemistry in 1973 for research into organo-metallic compounds.

Nevil Mott (1905–96; born in Leeds). Jointly awarded the Prize for Physics in 1977 for research into the properties of non-crystalline solids.

John Walker (born in 1941 in Halifax). Jointly awarded the Prize for Chemistry in 1997 for DNA research.

Oliver Smithies (born in 1925 in Halifax). Jointly awarded the Prize for Physiology or Medicine in 2007 for work in developing gene targeting.

ONE MAN AND HIS DOG

Sheep dogs are a familiar part of the Yorkshire dales, fields and fells all year round, but the best place to see them in action is at one of the county's many sheep dog trials.

Trials have been run in England since the 1870s, and Yorkshire has always been one of the sport's heartlands. To the uninitiated they can seem something of a, well, trial – but they are carefully organised events and precisely followed by competing dogs and their handlers. The basic idea is to get the dogs marshalling a group of sheep – usually about five – around a field via a series of fences, gates and enclosures. They begin by leaving their handler to fetch the sheep several hundred yards away then return with them, all the while following the handler's shouted or whistled instructions. Extra challenges may include separating one or more sheep from the pack, keeping as close as possible to a straight line, or driving sheep away from the handler – something that goes against dogs' instincts. The relationships between farmer, dog and sheep are fascinating to observe.

The trials are an excellent test of a dog's obedience and its skill in controlling sheep, and they are designed to replicate their working conditions on farms rather than make them perform any fancy tricks. Judges deduct points for any slip-ups along the way, with the highest aggregate score winning the event. Trials are keenly contested and were featured on the BBC's *One Man and His Dog* show for nearly 15 years until the late 1990s, helping to spread awareness of the sport across the country. Though participation isn't quite at the levels of its heyday in the 1950s, when thousands would watch events and hundreds would enter, Yorkshire trials still draw plenty of interest. Sheep dog trials are an important element of county shows like the Great Yorkshire

Show, while the International Sheep Dog Society, formed in 1906, organises 'National' trials in England, Scotland, Ireland and Wales. An 'International' event, held on even more demanding courses with many more sheep, decides the supreme sheep dog champion.

In Yorkshire as in most of England, sheep dogs are usually Border Collies. It can take months to train a dog properly, and skilful dogs from illustrious bloodlines are much sought after, for their skill on the farm as well as in competitions. The best can change hands at auction for several thousand pounds, though a good dog alone will not win trials for its owner. Much of the skill lies in the almost telepathic communication between a handler and his or her dog – and unlike some animal sports, this is an activity that the dogs clearly enjoy.

Sheep dog lingo ...

Away drive – herding sheep away from the handler rather than towards him

Bring – the act of returning sheep towards the handler or pen

Cast or **outrun** – a dog's run to retrieve the sheep

Cross drive – moving the sheep in a straight line in front of the handler

Eye-dog – a dog that can control sheep by its head movement alone

Lift – the act of retrieving the sheep; a *double lift* involves the retrieval of two separate groups of sheep

Penning – herding the sheep into a pen or enclosure

Shedding – separating some marked sheep from the group

Singling – separating one sheep from the group

Timed out – unable to complete the course in the allotted time

... and some sheep dog commands

Away – go anti-clockwise around the sheep

Balance – position so that the sheep move towards the handler

Come by – go clockwise around the sheep

Come or **here** – move towards the handler

Easy – slow down

Get back – retreat to give the sheep more room

Stand – stop and remain on feet

That'll do – stop and return

There – stop and wait for instructions

Walk up – move towards the sheep.

YORKSHIRE SAYINGS

Bradford for cash, Halifax for dash
Wakefield for pride and poverty;
Huddersfield for show, Sheffield for what's low
Leeds for dirt and vulgarity.
Birstall for ringers, Heckmondwike for singers,
Dewsbury for pedlars, Cleckheaton for sheddlers [swindlers].

TEN STATELY HOMES

Here are just ten of the many interesting historic houses dotted around Yorkshire, all of them open to the public.

Beningbrough Hall, near York. A National Trust-owned Georgian mansion with dozens of famous paintings thanks to links with the National Portrait Gallery. Tel. 01904 472027 or visit www.nationaltrust. org.uk.

Burton Agnes Hall, near Bridlington. An Elizabethan mansion stuffed with fine art, furniture and carvings, owned by the same family through 15 generations. Tel. 01262 490324 or visit www.burton-agnes.co.uk.

Burton Constable Hall, near Hull. An Elizabethan mansion built by the Constables, an important Yorkshire landowning family, with 300 acres (120 ha) of grounds. Tel. 01964 562400 or visit www.burtonconstable.com.

Castle Howard, near Malton. A magnificent 18th-century house that took a century to finish and has been restored since a fire in 1940. Attracts some 200,000 visitors a year. Tel. 01653 648444 or visit www.castlehoward.co.uk.

Duncombe Park, Helmsley. The elegant home of Lord and Lady Feversham near the North York Moors, recently refurbished and with substantial grounds. Tel. 01439 772625 or visit www.duncombe park.com.

Fairfax House, York. A Georgian townhouse built as a dowry for Anne Fairfax and restored in the 1980s by the York Civic Trust. It is full of magnificent furniture and decoration. Tel. 01904 655543 or visit www.fairfaxhouse.co.uk.

Harewood House, near Leeds. Built in the 18th century with money from the sugar trade and full of fine art and furniture. Home of the Queen's cousin, the Earl of Harewood. Tel. 0113 218 1010 or visit www.harewood.org.

Markenfield Hall, near Ripon. Built around 1280 but confiscated after the Rising of the North in 1569. Now back in private ownership, it is open on limited days or for organised tours. Tel. 01765 692303 or visit www.markenfield.com.

Newby Hall, near Ripon. Built in the 1690s and later expanded by the famous architect Robert Adam, the hall has what may be the biggest collection of chamber pots of any English house. Tel. 0845 450 4068 or visit www.newbyhall.co.uk.

Sledmere House, near Driffield. A mid-18th-century house in the Wolds, built by the Sykes family of Yorkshire traders. Gutted by a fire in 1911 but carefully restored since. Tel. 01377 236637 or visit www.sledmerehouse.com.

STRIKING IN YORKSHIRE DIALECT

Perhaps because of its long history of conflict over the centuries – or perhaps because some of its men enjoy a fight – the Yorkshire dialect has dozens of words for hitting. Here are some of the more original alternatives.

bang • bassock • belt • bensel • bolsh • bray • clap • clatter •
clawk • clonk • cloot • clout • cob • cotter • ding • dunch • fetch •
flup • jart • jowle • kelk • knap • knobble • lace • lam • land •
pawse • pay • ruddle • scuff • shelp • skelp • slug • threp • tipple •
twilt • wallop • wang • welt

HELL, HULL AND HALIFAX

Comparing Hull and Halifax to Hell is probably enough to get you sued for libel these days, but at one time wrongdoers had good reason to fear the towns.

The expression 'From Hell, Hull and Halifax deliver us' comes from John Taylor's poem 'The Beggar's Litany', sometimes known as 'The Thief's Litany'. When it was written in the early 17th century both Hull and Halifax had well-earned reputations for the strictness of their law enforcement - Hull for its infamous jail and Halifax for its enthusiasm for capital punishment as a public deterrent. Halifax's guillotine - the poem's 'jyn' or engine - would dispatch petty criminals after summary trials and was probably used to protect the town's developing cloth industry from criminals. The full Beggar's Litany reads:

> There is a proverb, and a prayer withall,
> That we may not to three strange places fall;
> From Hull, from Halifax, from Hell, 'tis thus,
> From all these three, Good Lord, deliver us.
> This praying Proverb's meaning to set down,
> Men do not wish deliverance from the Town;
> The town's named Kingston, Hull's the furious river;
> And from Halifax's dangers, I say Lord deliver.
> At Halifax, the law so sharp doth deal,
> That whoso more than 13 pence doth steal;
> They have a jyn that wondrous, quick and well,
> Sends thieves all headless unto Heaven or Hell.
> From Hell each man says Lord deliver me,
> Because from Hell can no redemption be.
> Men may escape from Hull and Halifax,
> But sure in Hell there is a heavier tax.
> Let each one for themselves in this agree,
> And pray - from Hell, Good Lord, deliver me.

YORKSHIRE'S HERITAGE IN NUMBERS

Figures for the Yorkshire and Humber region from English Heritage.

31,895 . . . . total listed buildings
2,673 . . . . Scheduled Ancient Monuments
1,482 . . . . Grade II listed buildings
784 . . . . Conservation Areas
683 . . . . Grade I listed buildings (the highest rating)
129 . . . . Buildings at Risk
121 . . . . registered parks and gardens
33 . . . . percentage of Scheduled Ancient Monuments classified as
being at 'high risk'

A DIARY OF FARMERS' MARKETS

Shoppers' appetite for locally produced food has triggered a huge increase in the number of farmers' markets across Yorkshire in the last few years. They are good news for farmers too, since trading direct with the public tends to provide them with a lot more profit than dealing through supermarkets. Yorkshire now boasts dozens of regular events, and they are all worth a visit to pick up some of the food that the region is famous for. Most of these markets run from 9 or 10 in the morning until early afternoon.

Cleckheaton – first Saturday of the month at St John's car park
Doncaster – first and third Wednesday of the month at Goosehill
Driffield – first Saturday of the month at Kelleythorpe showground
Easingwold – third Wednesday of the month on the Square
Grassington – third Sunday of the month in the village centre
Guisborough – first Sunday of the month at Pinchinthorpe Hall
Halifax – third Saturday of the month on Russell Street
Harrogate – second Thursday of the month on Cambridge Street
Hawes – second Saturday of the month on the Historic Quay
Hebden Bridge – first Saturday of the month on Lees Road
Holmfirth – third Sunday of the month in the Market Hall
Leeds – first and third Sunday of the month on Kirkgate
Leyburn – fourth Saturday of the month on Market Place
Malton – last Saturday of the month on Market Place
Northallerton – fourth Wednesday of the month on High Street
Otley – last Sunday of the month on Market Square
Pateley Bridge – fourth Sunday of the month at the Memorial Hall
Pickering – first Thursday of the month on Market Place
Pudsey – last Thursday of the month on Market Square
Richmond – third Saturday of the month in the Town Square
Ripon – third Sunday of the month in the Town Square
Saltaire – third Saturday of the month on Caroline Street
Selby – first Wednesday of the month outside the Abbey
Settle – second Sunday of the month on Town Square
Sheffield – fourth Sunday of the month at Barkers Pool
Skipton – first Sunday of the month on the Canal Basin
South Cave – second Saturday of the month on the school playground
Stokesley – first Saturday of the month on Town Square
Thirsk – second Monday of the month on Town Square
Wetherby – second Sunday of the month on Market Place
York – first and third Saturday of the month at York Auction Centre, and last Friday of the month on Parliament Street.

YORKSHIRE'S TOP TEN PLACES
BY POPULATION

In Leeds, Sheffield and Hull, Yorkshire has three of England's ten biggest cities by population, and another five places have 100,000 or more residents. Here are Yorkshire's top ten cities and towns by population, based on a breakdown of the 2001 census data by the Office for National Statistics' definition of 'urban areas'.

	City	Population at 2001 Census
1	Leeds	443,247
2	Sheffield	439,866
3	Hull	301,416
4	Bradford	293,717
5	Huddersfield	146,234
6	Middlesbrough	142,691
7	York	137,505
8	Rotherham	117,262
9	Harrogate and Knaresborough	85,128
10	Halifax	83,570

ENGLAND'S BIGGEST
WHITE HORSE

Yorkshire's claim that it has the biggest and best of everything is certainly true of its famous white horse at Kilburn.

There are several examples of this strange hillside art in the south of England, though none further north than Kilburn. The white horse at Uffington in Wiltshire is probably more widely known and is certainly much older, having probably been built in the Iron Age – but Yorkshire's just outdoes it in surface area. Cut into the hillside above Kilburn, not far from Thirsk on the edge of the North York Moors, it measures some 320 feet (97 m) from head to tail and 220 feet (67 m) from top to bottom. Close up, the horse is rather disappointing, its shape indistinguishable, but from a distance or from above, the sight is spectacular. It can be seen from the village below and across the Vale of York, and from passing roads and railway lines.

The horse was the idea of a successful local businessman, Thomas Taylor. Having seen Uffington's version in 1857, he decided that Yorkshire should have a hillside horse of its own – and, naturally, it had to be bigger. The shape was marked out by local pupils from an artist's drawing, before locals dug out the topsoil to expose the rock beneath. Most white horses around the country get their colour from the chalk hills they were built into, but the sandstone of Kilburn's version meant it needed some help with its colouring – an enormous and difficult task given that it covers more than an acre of steep hillside. Thirty men and six tons of lime were needed to create the right effect, and the labour must have been backbreaking.

Until a suitable waterproofing treatment is found, the horse is threatened by the vagaries of the Yorkshire weather, and it was nearly destroyed by hailstorms in 1896. The horse was neglected after the First World War, but a public appeal organised by the *Yorkshire Post* raised money to have it whitened and tidied up – only for it to have to be covered up during the Second World War to stop enemy pilots using it as a navigation guide. Since then, various volunteers have helped to maintain it, and it is now cared for by a charity, the Kilburn White Horse Association. The horse requires a lot of grooming, with the problems of erosion and fading colour demanding constant maintenance – and an awful lot of whitewash.

FAMOUS YORKSHIRE FOLK – JOSEPH ROWNTREE

To those old enough to recall it, the Rowntree name is probably best known for the range of chocolate bars and sweets manufactured under its brand. But in Yorkshire, and York in particular, Joseph Rowntree is better remembered as a philanthropist and social reformer who left as lasting a legacy as anyone on his home county.

Rowntree was born in York in 1836 and at 14 went to work in his father's grocery business. He later joined his brother at York's cocoa and chocolate factory, helping to transform it from a small family concern into a vast multinational empire. By the end of the 19th century it was one of Yorkshire's biggest manufacturing employers with about 4,000 workers.

Influenced by his family's Quaker values, Rowntree always had a strong awareness of his debt to society. After becoming sole owner of the factory on his brother's death, he started to construct grand community projects, building schools, libraries and war memorials in York. His factory provided better-than-average wages, basic healthcare and free education for young employees, and he introduced a pension fund and other benefits. Even by modern standards Rowntree's sense of corporate responsibility was considerable – but in his own time it was remarkable.

Looking beyond his own factory, Rowntree tried to explore ways of tackling poverty, funding research, books, newspapers and political campaigns to advance equality. In 1904 he gave about half of his wealth to set up various charitable trusts, known nowadays as the Joseph Rowntree Foundation, which funds research into the reasons for social problems like poverty and poor housing and possible solutions; the Joseph Rowntree Housing Trust, which offers affordable housing and runs care homes; the Joseph Rowntree Reform Trust, which supports progressive politics and social reform; and the Joseph Rowntree Charitable Trust, which champions Quaker ideals like peace and equality. The Rowntree name also lives on in schools and parks, and in 2000 readers of *York Press* newspaper voted him their 'Man of the Millennium'.

BRITAIN'S OTHER NATIONAL PARKS

Yorkshire takes in three of Britain's 14 National Parks – all of the Yorkshire Dales and the North York Moors, and a good chunk of the Peak District. Between them they share some 1,800 square miles (4,660 sq km) and 83,000 people. Here are the eleven other National Parks.

	Founded	Area in sq m (sq km)	Population
Peak District	**1951**	**555 (1,437)**	**38,000**
Lake District	1951	885 (2,292)	42,200
Snowdonia	1951	840 (2,176)	25,480
Dartmoor	1951	368 (953)	29,100
Pembrokeshire Coast	1952	240 (622)	22,800
North York Moors	**1952**	**554 (1,435)**	**25,500**
Yorkshire Dales	**1954**	**685 (1,774)**	**19,700**
Exmoor	1954	267 (692)	10,600
Northumberland	1956	405 (1,049)	2,200
Brecon Beacons	1957	519 (1,344)	32,000
The Broads	1989	117 (303)	5,700
Loch Lomond and the Trossachs	2002	720 (1,865)	15,600
Cairngorms	2003	1,467 (3,800)	16,000
The New Forest	2005	220 (570)	34,400

A 15th National Park, the South Downs, is awaiting designation pending the results of a public inquiry. The proposed Park has an area of 1,020 square miles (2,642 sq km) and a population of around 115,000.

YORKSHIREMEN IN THE RUGBY LEAGUE HALL OF FAME

Of the 17 players in English rugby league's official hall of fame, six were born in Yorkshire. Eligibility is restricted to those who played the sport in England for at least ten years and have been retired for at least five. Yorkshire's six, with their places of birth, are:

Billy Batten - Kinsley	**Roger Millward** - Castleford
Ellery Hanley - Leeds	**Jonty Parkin** - Sharlston
Neil Fox - Sharlston	**Harold Wagstaff** - Holmfirth

THE REAL CALENDAR GIRLS

If you've ever been persuaded to buy a risqué calendar featuring people from your town or village, you can blame a small Women's Institute group in Yorkshire.

The Rylstone WI branch conceived the idea of a calendar to raise money for Leukaemia Research and decided to broaden its appeal by getting its members to strip off - their modesty protected by strategically placed whisks and tea cups. As the story captured imaginations around the world, what began as a project to sell a few thousand copies ended with sales of more than 300,000 calendars.

The success alerted film companies, and in 2003 *Calendar Girls*, featuring Helen Mirren, Julie Walters and a host of other stars, became one of the most successful British films ever made. As well as raising even more money for Rylstone's charity, the movie was a great showcase for the Yorkshire Dales and has prompted a surge in tourism to some of the featured villages and dales. Scenes in the film's fictional village of Knapely were filmed in Kettlewell in Wharfedale, while Burnsall provided the set for the film's village fete. Kilnsey, Settle and Ilkley also served as locations for various scenes.

The Yorkshire Dales National Park has a leaflet to guide people around Calendar Girls country, available from Tourist Information Centres. The Rylstone group has meanwhile raised well over £1 million for its charity - and has given in to popular demand by stripping off for more calendars.

SOME YORKSHIRE RIVERS AND THEIR MEANINGS

Many of the rivers in Yorkshire are derived from Celtic words associated with water. Here are some of the principal rivers and their meanings.

Aire - from the Celtic word *isara*, meaning strong

Bain - probably from the Old Norse word *beinn*, meaning straight; the Bain is thought to be the shortest river in England, flowing for just 2 miles (3.2 km)

Calder - from the Celtic word *caled*, meaning hard or swift waters

Cover - the river in the hollow, derived from the Celtic word *cau*, meaning hollow

Derwent - from the Celtic word *derua*, meaning oak tree

Don - from the Celtic word *dana*, meaning water or stream

Dove - from the Celtic word *dubo*, meaning dark or black

Esk - from the Celtic word *isca*, meaning water or stream

Nidd - from the Celtic word *nouijos*, meaning bright

Ouse - from the Celtic word *usa*, meaning water

Ribble - from the Celtic goddess of water, Reigh Belisama

Rother - probably derived from *rud wbr*, meaning red water

Swale - from the Anglo-Saxon word for rushing or whirling; the Swale is one of the fastest flowing rivers in the country

Tees - from the Celtic word *teis*, meaning surging water

Ure - from the Celtic word *isura*, meaning the holy one

Wharfe - derived from both Celtic and Old Norse words meaning winding river

YORKSHIRE CCC'S TWENTY CRICKET GROUNDS

Yorkshire County Cricket Club has played first-class cricket at 20 different grounds around the county in the century and a half since its first match. At times Yorkshire would take their games all around the county, but falling attendances and rising costs of staging fixtures means the number of grounds has dwindled. Half of the 20 venues have not been played on since the 19th century, but many others were employed until relatively recently, and their names are a nostalgic roll-call of Yorkshire cricket through the years. Of the 20 grounds, Yorkshire now hosts first-class fixtures at only two. With the year of the last game played there, the grounds are:

Headingley, Leeds – to present

North Marine Road, Scarborough – to present

Park Avenue, Bradford – 1996

St George's Road, Harrogate – 1996

Acklam Park, Middlesbrough – 1996

Abbeydale Park, Sheffield – 1996

The Circle, Hull – 1974

Bramall Lane, Sheffield – 1973

Fartown, Huddersfield – 1955

Dewsbury and Savile Ground, Dewsbury – 1933

Thrum Hall, Halifax – 1897

Wigginton Road, York – 1890

Recreation Ground, Holbeck – 1886

Hall Park, Horsforth – 1885

Linthorpe Road West, Middlesbrough – 1882

Town Ground, Hull – 1879

College Grove, Wakefield – 1878

Great Horton Road, Bradford – 1874

Woodhouse Hill, Hunslet – 1869

Swatter's Carr, Middlesbrough – 1867

YORKSHIRE FOOD – WENSLEYDALE CHEESE

Crumbly, moist and slightly sweet, Wensleydale is now one of the most popular types of cheeses in the country – and yet it may owe its survival to a couple of cartoon characters.

Cheese is thought to have been made in Wensleydale since the 12th century. As with many foods and drinks, it was monks who were the pioneers – in this case French Cistercians producing cheese from their monastery in the dale. The lush limestone meadows of Wensleydale are thought to be behind the distinctive taste of the cheese, and though it is now made from cow's milk and eaten very young, the monks' version was probably a bluer cheese from ewes' milk, matured for a long time in the monastery's cool cellar.

After the dissolution of the monasteries in the 16th century, cheese production became a cottage industry among the farming communities of Wensleydale. From the late 19th century, production became rather more organised, with milk from farmers across the dale going to a central creamery at Hawes for cheese production. In the 1960s the creamery was bought by the Milk Marketing Board, and though the cheese remained popular, rising costs and competition led it in the early 1990s to suggest moving production out of the dale – and, to the disgust of all Yorkshire, over the border into Lancashire. Rather than see the cheese leaving the county, managers bought out the creamery and relaunched the Wensleydale brand.

The creamery has thrived ever since, providing income for dozens of local farmers as well as employment in its cheese production, which continues to be done by hand. Its success owes a great deal to the animated characters Wallace and Gromit who, just after the buyout, endorsed the cheese in their films because their animators liked the name. Sales went through the roof when the creamery agreed a deal to launch a Wallace and Gromit cheese, and coming as it did amid difficult market conditions, the association may have saved the business.

The Hawes creamery has always claimed to be the only true and proper producer of Yorkshire Wensleydale cheese and is now campaigning for protected status from the European Union. As it does with products like Parmesan and Champagne, that would stop producers hundreds of miles from Wensleydale from using its name on their cheeses. Closer to home in Yorkshire, meanwhile, plenty of other smaller cheese makers are also flourishing after a revival of interest in traditional types of cheese.

YORKSHIRE'S ARCHBISHOP

In the hierarchy of the Church of England the Archbishop of York ranks second in importance only to the Archbishop of Canterbury. He guides the work of the diocese of York, which once covered most of northern England but which nowadays stretches from the River Tees down to the Humber, taking in 602 churches and 127 schools across 469 Yorkshire parishes. Helping the Archbishop are the Bishops of Hull, Selby and Whitby and the Archdeacons of York, Cleveland and the East Riding.

The Archbishop of York is also known as the Primate of England and Metropolitan, and of the Province of York, which covers all the dioceses in the north of England. (The Archbishop of Canterbury trumps York's title with the role of Primate of All England.) His throne is at York Minster, and his official residence since 1241 is Bishopthorpe Palace near York.

There have been 97 Archbishops of York since the post was established in 627, and while the role does not now bring with it quite the influence over state matters it had in the past, it is nevertheless an important and influential position. The current incumbent – and the first non-white person ever to take up the role – is John Sentamu, who was born in Uganda in 1949. Sentamu studied law in his home country but was imprisoned for speaking out against the country's brutal dictator Idi Amin in the 1970s. Fleeing to Britain, he studied theology at Cambridge University before training as a priest. After several inner-city parish roles he became Bishop of Stepney in 1996 and Bishop of Birmingham in 2002. Impressing there, he was recommended for York when David Hope left to take up a role in a Yorkshire parish, and he was enthroned in November 2005 at a lively ceremony in York Minster featuring African music and dancing.

Sentamu has since continued what for an Archbishop of York is an unorthodox and forthright but highly engaging and all-inclusive style. He has always campaigned against racism, crime and social injustice, and in 2006 he staged a sit-in in a tent by the altar at York Minster, fasting and praying for seven days to demonstrate against the ongoing conflict in the Middle East. In 2007 he protested against the regime of Robert Mugabe in Zimbabwe by cutting up his dog collar and refusing to wear it again until Mugabe left his post.

Sentamu was voted Yorkshire Man of the Year in 2007 and, accepting the award, emphasised his Yorkshire credentials by pointing out that, spelt backwards, one of his Ugandan names, Mugabi, reads 'ee bah gum'. He is also a patron and season ticket holder at York City football club, prompting fellow fans to joke that his faith must be truly bottomless.

Five more interesting Archbishops of York

Saint Paulinus (627–633). The first known incumbent after the building of York Minster in 627, though technically his correct title was Bishop of York rather than Archbishop of York.

Richard le Scrope (1398–1407). Executed in York for treason against Henry IV.

Thomas Wolsey (1514–1530). The Archbishop of York for 16 years, even though he never actually came to the city. After travelling as far as Cawood Castle to prepare for his enthronement, he was arrested for treason on the orders of Henry VIII and died soon afterwards.

Edward Venables Vernon Harcourt (1807-1847). In the post for 40 years, making him the longest serving archbishop of the last 700 years (Wulfhere managed 46 years from 854 to 900, and Walter de Grey 40 from 1215 to 1255.)

William Connor Magee (1891). The shortest serving archbishop of modern times, he died four months after his appointment.

THE TOURIST HOTSPOTS

Room occupancy rates give a fairly reliable indication of the popularity or otherwise of destinations. These figures, based on Yorkshire Tourist Board's survey of hoteliers' rates in the various districts of the area, show that Harrogate has seen the biggest rise in room occupancy over the last ten years - suggesting that the spa town is an increasingly popular draw for tourists. Ryedale, spanning the North York Moors and the Wolds, has also steadily pulled in more visitors. Oddly, bottom of the list is York, which, despite continuing to pull in city break visitors, has seen room occupancy rates fall by more than 8 per cent in the last ten years - though this, of course, could also indicate an increase in the number of rooms available.

	Occupancy rate	Ten-year change in rate
Harrogate	69.4	+ 16.3
Ryedale	55.4	+ 12.9
Rotherham	65.3	+ 5.0
Hambleton	51.1	+ 5.0
Craven	54.7	+ 4.7
Richmondshire	52.2	+ 4.6
East Riding	55.0	+ 3.6
Calderdale	55.2	+ 1.7
Sheffield	61.6	+ 1.3
Leeds	66.0	+ 0.6
Scarborough	55.8	- 1.3
Doncaster	62.0	- 7.1
Bradford	54.1	- 7.6
Kirklees	50.3	- 7.6
York	59.1	- 8.4

A BRONTË TRAIL

Yorkshire's Brontë connections pull in thousands of literary tourists each year. Most of them flock to the family home at Haworth, and the towns, villages and moorland around it in west Yorkshire and over into Lancashire are now so closely associated with the sisters that it is commonly called Brontë Country. But the links stretch well beyond this patch of Yorkshire. Here are ten places to learn more about Anne, Charlotte and Emily.

The Brontë Birthplace, Market Street, Thornton. This is where all the sisters were born. The future of the building is currently uncertain as it was sold to a private developer in 2007.

Brontë Parsonage Museum, Haworth. The top Brontë attraction, the parsonage was where the sisters lived, grew up and wrote most of their novels. Now looked after by the Brontë Society. Tel. 01535 642323 or visit www.bronte.info.

St Michael's and All Angels Church, Haworth. The church of Patrick Brontë while the family lived at the parsonage. It is home to the family vault where Emily and Charlotte are buried.

Top Withens, near Haworth. The ruined, weather-beaten and atmospheric farmstead is usually accepted as the inspiration for the Earnshaw moorland farm in Emily Brontë's *Wuthering Heights*. On the way up from Haworth is the Brontë Waterfall.

Oakwell Hall and Country Park, Batley. Visited by Charlotte and featured in her novel *Shirley*. Well preserved and open to the public. Tel. 01274 326240.

Ponden Hall, Stanbury. The inspiration for Thrushcross Grange in Emily Brontë's *Wuthering Heights*. Now privately owned.

Norton Conyers Hall, near Haworth. A fine 14th-century house, which was visited by Charlotte and was the place that inspired Thornfield Hall and the mad woman in the attic in *Jane Eyre*. Privately owned but sometimes open to the public. Tel. 01765 640333.

Red House Museum, Gomersal. The house of Charlotte's friend Mary Taylor and now a museum with material on the Brontë connections. Tel. 01274 335100.

St Mary's Church, Scarborough. Anne Brontë loved Scarborough and is buried in the graveyard here.

Cliff House, Filey. Where Charlotte lived after Anne's death, now marked by a blue plaque.

<hr />

FELL-RUNNING

If you're out walking in the Yorkshire hills and dales, there's a chance you'll encounter the hardiest of the county's human breeds – the fell-runner.

This is a sport that pushes competitors to the edge of their endurance, no matter how fit they are. Uphill, fell-running is a test of stamina that leaves runners gasping for breath and many reduced to a crawl on all fours. Coming down again it's more a test of skill, the best runners moving in virtual freefall, picking their way over the rocks and grass like mountain goats and trusting to natural instincts to get them to the bottom safely – all the while trying to overtake one another. Twisted ankles and broken bones are common as runners fly down so fast that they cover a mile in a couple of moments. To the bemused walker overtaken either by a wheezing fell-runner staggering up or a terrified-looking runner tumbling down, the appeal of the sport can seem rather mysterious – but it's a great way of seeing the hills and dales.

Yorkshire competes with the Lake District for the right to call itself the home of the sport of fell-running. The Lakes has the higher fells and the longer routes, but Yorkshire claims to have the tougher terrain and hardier runners. Both have well-organised fell-running clubs and communities and plenty of famous races, from short, sharp dashes to the top of a fell and back to marathons over several ranges and dales. Most take place in the spring or summer, but some claim that the snows and freezing temperatures of winter bring the races that separate the sport's real stars from the also-rans.

Yorkshire has a fell-running championship made up of a series of races over the year, and it's open to anyone born in the county or living there permanently for at least nine months. The flagship event is the Three Peaks race in April, run since 1954 and covering 24 miles (39 km) in distance and 4,550 feet (1,400 m) in mostly steep ascent over the Dales fells of Pen-y-Ghent, Ingleborough and Whernside. The course record time for men is 2 hours 46 minutes. The fell race is also a key part of many Yorkshire shows and sports days from as far back as the mid-19th century.

Since races criss-cross sizeable swathes of Yorkshire, runners have to be outstanding navigators as well as athletes, especially in the mists that can shroud the tops, and it is sometimes experienced locals rather than more talented outsiders who make it home first. But while winning is important to some, it is not really the point of fell-running. Even in the top races, prize money is modest and media coverage non-existent beyond the local papers of the north, so few run for the glamour. For most, fell-running is as much about enjoying Yorkshire's magnificent, rugged landscape as it is about competition or keeping fit.

YORKSHIRE POEMS

'I'm Yorkshire Too' – ANONYMOUS

By t'side of a brig, that stands over a brook,
    I was sent betimes to school;
I went wi' the stream, as I studied my book,
    An' was thought to be no small fool.
I never yet bought a pig in a poke,
    For, to give awd Nick his due,
Tho' oft I've dealt wi' Yorkshire folk,
    Yet I was Yorkshire too.

I was pretty well lik'd by each village maid,
    At races, wake or far,
For my father had addled a vast in trade,
    And I were his son and heir.
And seeing that I didn't want for brass,
    Poor girls came first to woo,
But tho' I delight in a Yorkshire lass,
    Yet I was Yorkshire too!

To Lunnon by father I was sent,
    Genteeler manners to see;
But fashion's so dear, I came back as I went,
    And so they made nothing o'me.
My kind relations would soon have found out
    · What was best wi' my money to do:
Says I, 'My dear cousins, I thank ye for nowt,
    But I'm not to be cozen'd by you!
        For I'm Yorkshire too.'

YORKSHIRE MUSICIANS

Twenty-five singers, songwriters, groups and composers from Yorkshire, with their place of birth or, in bands' cases, formation.

The Arctic Monkeys – Sheffield	Bruce Dickinson – Sheffield
Mel B – Leeds	Embrace – Brighouse
Janet Baker – Hatfield	Gang of Four – Leeds
John Barry – York	Human League – Sheffield
Josephine Barstow – Sheffield	Kaiser Chiefs – Leeds
The Beautiful South – Hull	Lesley Garrett – Thorne
Arthur Brown – Whitby	Gareth Gates – Bradford
Tony Christie – Conisbrough	Robert Palmer – Batley
Joe Cocker – Sheffield	Pulp – Sheffield
John Curwen – Heckmondwike	Corinne Bailey Rae – Leeds
Kiki Dee – Bradford	Chris Rea – Middlesbrough
Def Leppard – Sheffield	Kate Rusby – Barnsley
Frederick Delius – Bradford	

TEN GARDENS

Yorkshire has dozens of wonderful gardens, some of them part of magnificent country house estates and others stand-alone designs. All of the following are open to the public, though hours are sometimes limited.

Burnby Hall Gardens, near Pocklington. There are 8 acres (3.2 ha) of garden around two lakes, including the national collection of hardy water lilies. Tel. 01759 307125 or visit www.burnbyhallgardens.com.

Castle Howard, near Malton. A thousand acres (405 ha) of parkland with walled, vegetable and woodland gardens, plus temples, statues and follies dotted around. Tel. 01653 648444 or visit www.castlehoward.co.uk.

Constable Burton Hall Gardens, near Bedale. The 18th-century parklands have a large romantic garden and annual tulip festival. Tel. 01677 450428 or visit www.constableburtongardens.co.uk.

Helmsley Walled Garden. The 18th-century gardens were neglected until recently but are now being restored, with ranges including 50 or so Yorkshire apple varieties. Tel. 01439 771427 or visit www.helmsley walledgarden.org.uk.

RHS Garden Harlow Carr, near Harrogate. The varied and seasonally changing gardens of the Royal Horticultural Society. Tel. 01423 565418 or visit www.rhs.org.uk/harlowcarr.

Rievaulx Terrace, near Helmsley. Landscaped gardens and terraces hosting Georgian temples on National Trust-owned land. Tel. 01439 798340 or visit www.nationaltrust.org.uk.

Sheffield Botanical Gardens. There are 15 garden areas, including some rare collections, plus listed pavilions, recently restored. Tel. 0114 268 6001 or visit www.sbg.org.uk.

Studley Royal Water Garden, near Ripon. An 18th-century water garden was inspired by the French landscapers of the time, now, with Fountains Abbey, a World Heritage site. Tel. 01765 608888 or visit www.fountainsabbey.org.uk.

The Walled Garden at Scampston Hall, near Malton. Acclaimed and innovative walled country house garden, plus woodland walks and parkland. Tel. 01944 759111 or visit www.scampston.co.uk.

Wentworth Castle Gardens, near Barnsley. A Grade I listed parkland, newly restored after the recovery of lost gardens and the planting of 100,000 bulbs. Tel. 01226 776040 or visit www.wentworthcastle.org.

FAMOUS YORKSHIRE FOLK – AMY JOHNSON

Amy Johnson was a pioneering aviator who set new standards of achievement for pilots as well as for women of her time – done with a striking, single-minded determination characteristic of Yorkshire.

Johnson was born in Hull in 1903, and – fairly unusually for a woman of her time – studied and graduated at the University of Sheffield. Even more unusually, she then took up flying as a hobby, buying her first plane with the help of her prosperous father and some sponsors. In 1930, less than a year after her first solo flight and aged just 26, Johnson set her first and most famous record – flying from Britain to Australia. The 10,000 mile (16,090 km) journey took nearly three weeks, and while others had completed it more quickly, Johnson was the first woman to do it solo. Having previously flown no further than from London to Hull, the achievement was remarkable, and Johnson captured the public's imagination at a time when explorers were opening up the world. She was feted across Australia and Britain, where thousands greeted her return, and was showered with numerous medals, honours and gifts.

Nothing was likely to better this achievement, but Johnson went on to complete plenty more long-distance records. She become the first pilot to fly from London to Moscow in a day, and set new marks for flights to Japan, South Africa and India. Some of her records were set in joint flights with Jim Mollison, a famous pilot with whom she had a short-lived marriage, but it was for her flights alone that she gained the greatest fame. During the Second World War Johnson joined the Air Transport Auxiliary to ferry planes around RAF bases, and she died in 1941 after baling out of a plane she was flying from Blackpool to Oxford in bad weather. Partly because her body was never found, there has been some speculation that her plane may have been shot down, either by German fighters or British anti-aircraft guns, or that a mysterious other person was on board with her at the time.

Johnson is remembered in Hull by a statue, and after her return from Australia she created an annual award for acts of courage by the town's children that is still given in the city. Sewerby Hall near Bridlington has a room of Johnson memorabilia donated by her family. The Gipsy Moth plane used for her flight to Australia is now in the Science Museum in London.

WHERE FOOTBALL KICKED OFF

Though it hasn't enjoyed a great deal of top-flight success in the last few decades, Yorkshire can at least lay claim to being the home of football.

Although there are sketchy records of some semi-organised clubs going back further, football bodies like FIFA and the FA recognise Sheffield FC as the world's oldest surviving club. Records show that it was officially formed on 24 October 1857, when players from the city's cricket club decided to kick a ball about to while away the long winter months. It marked out its first ground on a field on Sheffield's East Bank Road and used a nearby potting shed as its headquarters.

Being the first club, Sheffield had to provide its own opposition, breaking up its members into married elevens versus single men, or professional occupations against 'the rest'. It also had to devise some rules, and the set it came up with – the 'Sheffield Rules' – helped to transform football from a chaotic activity into a more organised and orderly sport. Sheffield claims responsibility for numerous things that are now part and parcel of football – crossbars, free kicks, throw-ins and even heading the ball.

Football's popularity spread fast. Within five years there were a dozen more clubs in Sheffield and the original club was travelling further afield to play fixtures. Its influence in the game soon waned, the Football Association in London establishing itself as the game's rule-maker and regulator, and the dawn of professionalism left the staunchly amateur Sheffield FC further behind. The club dropped down the leagues but has now played continuously for more than 150 years on various grounds around the city, most recently in the Dronfield area.

By rights, football's oldest club should also be one of its biggest and most successful, but things aren't quite that glamorous for the current Sheffield FC. While the city's United and Wednesday are in the top few tiers of the national game, Sheffield FC plays its football in the UniBond League Division One South. The club has used its status as the world's oldest to start a recruitment drive for more members, attracting several celebrity supporters and helping to secure its future.

CRICKETERS ON YORKSHIRE

'In an England cricket eleven, the flesh may be of the South, but the bone is of the North, and the backbone is Yorkshire.'
LEN HUTTON

'I would have died for Yorkshire. I suppose once or twice I nearly did.'
BRIAN CLOSE

'Don't tell me his average or his top score at Trent Bridge. How many runs, how many wickets did he get against Yorkshire?'
DOUGLAS JARDINE ON HIS METHODS FOR SELECTING PLAYERS FOR ENGLAND

YORKSHIRE INDUSTRY – TEXTILES

The 'dark satanic mills' of William Blake's famous verse 'Jerusalem' are an enduring image of post-Industrial Revolution northern England for many people. And the rise and fall of Yorkshire's textile mills tells in particular an important element of the history of the western side of the county over the last few centuries.

While Lancashire made its reputation and money out of cotton, Yorkshire concentrated on wool, and the way its products were traditionally manufactured for many years was a far cry from those dark satanic mills. The county's rich supply of sheep's wool meant weavers could use their handlooms or spinning wheels to produce more woollen items than they needed for their own use, the excess sold on via intermediaries. But the Industrial Revolution from the late 18th century onwards changed all that. As Yorkshire discovered new spinning machinery and looms, the industry was transformed, vastly increasing its efficiency and capacity. Yorkshire became the weaving capital of the world, with wool at one time accounting for up to a quarter of all British exports.

What was previously quite literally a cottage industry was now very different, run from vast, noisy mills where conditions were usually miserable and sometimes lethal. Mills sprung up across the West Riding, and the association with the rag trade of places like Batley, Bradford, Halifax, Huddersfield, Keighley, Shipley and Skipton means they are still referred to as mill towns. But while they made fortunes for a handful of mill owners and textile barons, the exponential rate of expansion often led to dreadful conditions in the cramped housing that was thrown up to cater for workers.

Almost as quickly as it grew, the wool business slumped. Like many traditional British industries, Yorkshire's textiles were hit by cheaper imports and the changing demands of the public, and a failure to invest in new technologies left its mills vulnerable to competition. After a temporary boost to production in the Second World War, mills began to shut or merge at an increasing rate. Though a few modern textile manufacturers remain, hoping to outdo their rivals with quality, service and the cachet of 'Made in Britain' branding, the industry is a fraction of what it once was in size and importance.

Textiles' rise and fall is encapsulated by the story of Salt's Mill in Bradford. Built and opened by Titus Salt in the 1850s, it was the centrepiece of an industrial village, Saltaire, which provided its workers with facilities and employment standards far beyond those common at the time. It was the biggest factory in the world, employing some 3,000 workers and turning out 30,000 metres of cloth a day. But output gradually declined and jobs were shed until, in 1986, it closed altogether.

Many old mills have been transformed into more modern business centres or trendy apartment blocks, and in Salts' case it was rescued from dereliction by a bold plan to turn it into a centre for art, leisure and business, with a large collection of work by Bradford artist David Hockney. Saltaire's streets and buildings offer an evocative glimpse of Yorkshire's industrial past, and the village is now a World Heritage Site. Other places to find out more about the history of Yorkshire's rag trade include Armley Mills in Leeds, once an enormous wool mill and now an industrial museum.

YORKSHIRE FELL AND CAVE RESCUE IN NUMBERS

Some statistics gathered by the Cave Rescue Organisation since it was formed in 1935 to rescue walkers and cavers in the Dales. For more information on the CRO and to make donations to help it continue its work, visit www.cro.org.uk.

3,061	people involved in incidents
2,042	incidents attended
702	fell incidents
620	cave incidents
217	lambs involved in incidents
193	sheep involved in incidents
87	age in years of the oldest person involved
85	climbing incidents
66	dogs involved in incidents
14	disused mine incidents
9	cows involved in incidents
5	age in months of the youngest person involved
1	cat involved in incidents

INSULTS AND EXCLAMATIONS IN YORKSHIRE DIALECT

Yorkshire's distinctive dialect has plenty of words and phrases that can be used as insults and exclamations. Here are some of the most interesting.

barm-pot – idiotic person • beltikite – good for nothing •
bon! – burn (in Hell) • booan idle – lazy • by 'eck – by hell •
by gum! or by Gow! – by God •
cack-'anded – clumsy (also left-handed) • callit – a nagging woman •
chump – fool • claht-'ead – cloth-head, stupid •
common-ossity – person of bad taste • deng – damn •
donnat – idler • dooad – fool • doughy – stupid • drat – bother •
feckless – useless • funny-ossity – strange person •
gammerstang – an immoral woman • gawp-'ead – stupid person •
gobby – loudmouthed • gommerill – fool • gormless – unintelligent •
hell fire! – goodness me • loopy – crazy • maddlin – fool •
maunsell – lazy woman • near – tight-fisted •

neither use nor ornament – useless • nip-screw – miser •
numb-yed – fool • nuppit – simpleton • slack-jack – lazy person •
stoddy – foolish • what the hummer! – what the hell

YORKSHIRE'S WORST PLACE TO LIVE

Yorkshire has the two worst places to live in the UK, according to a 2007 survey. A ranking organised by Channel 4's *Location Location Location* property programme put **Middlesbrough** top of the list of undesirable places, followed by **Hull**. The survey considered data on education, income, crime levels and drug and health problems among other things. Needless to say, the news was met with surprise and derision from Middlesbrough residents and civic leaders. **Doncaster** was the only other Yorkshire town to make the top 20.

HOW TO BUILD A CAIRN

All walkers in Yorkshire will have encountered cairns, used either to mark the summits of fells or to help guide people up and down them. They can be useful landmarks, especially when the mist descends and visibility reduces. Many walkers follow the tradition of adding stones to cairns as they pass them, and some on popular routes have accumulated large piles. Occasionally much neater assemblies can be found – and here's how the professional dry stone wallers build them.

Find the right position. Cairns need a firm base, which should be easy to find on rocky hilltops.

Get your stones. Good cairns need good materials. They also need more stones than it appears, since not all of them will be suitable.

Assemble your base. Plot a circular outline for the base. The outer base ring of the cairn needs the largest stones, with the widest ends of them to the outside. The middle of the base – or 'heart' of the cairn – is filled with smaller stones or other debris.

Build upwards. Add stones slowly, walking around the cairn to inspect progress and trying to keep each layer as flat and tight as possible.

Top it off. As the layers become tighter, use smaller or triangular stones on the layers. The final top stone should be larger.

ON THE TRAIL OF HEARTBEAT

After *Last of the Summer Wine* and *All Creatures Great and Small*, the third most popular TV series to come out of Yorkshire is probably *Heartbeat*. Like the two shows that came before it, *Heartbeat* found the winning formula of easygoing entertainment with plenty of lovely Yorkshire views, and it has notched up more than 300 episodes since it was first screened in 1992, with no sign of it running out of steam.

Set in the 1960s, the series features the goings-on of north Yorkshire villages, and in particular the lives of police officers trying to keep up with a phenomenally high crime rate. Like *All Creatures Great and Small*, it was originally based on books, in this instance the 'Constable' series by Peter Walker under the pseudonym of Nicholas Rhea, though it soon exhausted the supply of storylines and had to develop increasingly ambitious plots of its own. Entering its 17th series in 2008, it has also been syndicated all over the world, making for a rather odd introduction to Yorkshire for many people in far-flung corners of the world.

It's not difficult to find Heartbeat's real-life Yorkshire locations. The series' fictional homes of Aidensfield and Ashfordly are based on the villages of Goathland and Grosmont in the North York Moors. Much of the filming is done in Goathland, and the church, station and school are all adapted for use. Other regular locations include the Goathland Hotel (the Aidensfield Arms on screen), the Post Office (Aidensfield Stores) and Glendale House (Dr Ferrenby's surgery), which offers bed and breakfast accommodation to wide-eyed *Heartbeat* fans. Every time filming begins again, Goathland is transformed by TV crews back to the 1960s, with all signs of modern life and *Heartbeat* souvenirs tucked well out of sight.

The series also uses other locations around the North York Moors and beyond – police buildings are located miles away in Askwith and Otley, and much interior filming is now done in studios in Leeds. But just as Holmfirth and Thirsk have become known as the capitals of *Last of the Summer Wine* and *All Creatures Great and Small*, so Goathland has become the most important place of pilgrimage for thousands of *Heartbeat* viewers each year. Many arrive on the North Yorkshire Moors Railway, a picturesque steam line from Pickering to Whitby, and several agencies offer guided tours of the village. There is even a book – *Heartbeat Country* (Discovery Guides) – to help viewers track down every last Yorkshire location. Given that the series has averaged 20 shows a year since it started, there's a good chance that a summer visit will coincide with filming.

THE YEAR IN YORKSHIRE SHEEP FARMING

The calendar of Yorkshire's upland sheep is the story of the farmer's year too. Here's what happens when.

November	Mating between ewes and rams
December – January	Ewes return to the hills
February – March	Ewes, especially those carrying twins, may be returned to the low ground for extra feeding and observation
April	All ewes brought down from the hills and lambing begins
May	Ewes with single lambs go back up to the hills; those with twins or more stay in the enclosures
June – July	Ewes sheared, dipped and marked
August – September	Lambs weaned off their ewes; wether lambs (castrated males) sold or fattened for sale
October	Gimmer lambs (young females) go to winter on the lowlands

THE NEW GARDEN OF ENGLAND

Yorkshire residents have always argued that theirs is God's own county – but it can also now claim to be the garden of England too.

The title was always unofficially held by Kent, which has energetically promoted itself as such since the phrase was first coined in Henry VIII's time after he enjoyed some particularly good fruit from there. But a poll of 4,000 people by UKTV returned North Yorkshire as England's most beautiful county, based on criteria like the quality of countryside, villages and wildlife. It got 31.1 per cent of the vote, well clear of Devon and Derbyshire in second and third, with Kent pushed back to fifth place.

BRITAIN'S BLOODIEST BATTLE

As the list of battles elsewhere in this book shows, Yorkshire has a bloody history—but no conflict was as brutal as the 15th century Battle of Towton. Estimates of its casualties vary enormously, but many historians think this was the single most savage fight ever held on British soil.

The Wars of the Roses—between the Lancastrians under Henry VI and the Yorkists under Richard, Duke of York—had been running for several years by the time of Towton. They had intensified in 1460 when Henry, captured by Richard's men, agreed to remove his son as heir to the throne in favour of Richard. But spurred on by his wife, Margaret, Henry's Lancastrians fought on, first killing Richard and then recapturing Henry in successive battles. Richard's son Edward took up the Yorkists' cause and was crowned King by the influential 'Kingmaker' the Earl of Warwick in London in early March 1461.

With two men now claiming the crown, a climactic battle was inevitable. After several skirmishes nearby, the Yorkists and Lancastrians converged at Towton, just south of Tadcaster, on 29th March 1641. On snowy open fields, the battle raged for ten hours, and its importance meant that no quarter was given on either side. The fighting was ferocious. Though the Lancastrians had started from a strong position, a reinforcement of Yorkist numbers gave them the upper hand later in the day. Pushed back to the nearby river, the Lancastrians were routed and ruthlessly pursued as they fled.

Some records of the time put the number of men killed at Towton as high as 40,000, though that probably exaggerates the intensity of the fight. But even a mid-estimate of 20,000 men killed—perhaps around one in four of those who fought, and close to 1% of all Englishmen living at the time—makes it just about the bloodiest single day in the country's history. Strategically it was undoubtedly a significant battle, securing the throne for the Yorkist side and badly damaging the Lancastrian cause, though Henry and his wife and son were not present and escaped.

Much of the site of the Battle of Towton is still agricultural land, though it has been sliced up by enclosures and roads. There is a small memorial, and the river that trapped the Lancastrians still runs nearby, while recent excavation has uncovered mass graves from the battlefield.

THE STORIES OF YORK'S STREETS

The streets, snickelways, yards, bars and gates of York tell the rich history of the city, and in particular the professions of the people who have lived there over the centuries. Rather confusingly, York's gates are not gateways to the city – they are called bars – but streets, from the Old Norse word *gata*. Here is a guide to thirty of the more interesting place-names across York.

Bootham – probably refers to the market booths that once stood by this gate to the city

Colliergate – where coal or charcoal was traded

Coppergate – the street where metal workers and joiners worked

Davygate – named after David le Lardiner, 12th-century clerk of a kitchen

Feasegate – from the Old English for cow house street

Fishergate – where fishermen sold their catches

Fossgate – takes its name from the River Foxx

Gillygate – borrows its name from the Church of St Giles that once stood here

Goodramgate – from the Viking name Guthrum

Grape Lane – 'grape' originally meant grope, so it's not difficult to imagine what once went on here

Hornpot Lane – where the horn-workers lived

Hungate – the street where hounds were kept

Jubbergate – the area where Jews settled in the city

Knavesmire – the place where knaves and criminals were executed

Lendal – from the nearby St Leonard's Hospital that once stood here

Mad Alice Lane – now known more prosaically as Lund's Court, this is where a woman was hanged in the 19th century

Marygate – from St Mary's Abbey

Micklegate – meaning 'great street'

Monkgate – the monks who provided the name are unknown

Nessgate - *ness* is Old Norse for headland; here between the Rivers Foss and Ouse

Ousegate - from the River Ouse

Petergate - from the nearby Minster, dedicated to St Peter

Shambles - York's most famous street; the name comes from Flesh Shambles, old stalls from which meat was sold

Skeldergate - from the Old Norse for shield-maker

Spurriergate - where spur makers worked

St Saviourgate - from the church of the same name

Stonegate - paved street, perhaps dating back to Roman times

Swinegate - where swine were kept

Walmgate - probably named for a man called Walba or similar

Whip-Ma-Whop-Ma-Gate - the longest street name in York but probably its shortest in length; derived from the whipping post here in medieval times

YORKSHIRE'S BEST HOUSES

Simon Jenkins's encyclopaedic book England's *Thousand Best Houses* contains 92 places in Yorkshire - a fair ratio given the wealth of houses in the county, especially in the north. On Jenkins's star rating system, 25 get either three, four or the maximum five stars. They are:

Five stars
Burton Agnes Hall, near Bridlington
Castle Howard, near Malton
Harewood House, near Leeds

Four stars
Beningbrough Hall, near York
Burton Constable Hall, near Hull
Fairfax House, York
Newby Hall, near Ripon
Nostell Priory, near Wakefield

Three stars

Bolton Castle, near Leyburn

Broughton Hall, near Skipton

Duncombe Park, Helmsley

East Riddlesden Hall, Keighley

Hovingham Hall, Hovingham

Markenfield Hall, near Ripon

Merchant Adventurers' Hall, York

Newburgh Priory, near Helmsley

Norton Conyers, near Ripon

Nunnington Hall, Nunnington

Ripley Castle, Ripley

Shibden Hall, Halifax

Skipton Castle, Skipton

Sutton Park, Sutton-in-the-Forest

Sledmere House, near Driffield

Temple Newsam, near Leeds

Treasurer's House, York

FAMOUS YORKSHIRE FOLK – HENRY MOORE AND BARBARA HEPWORTH

Born within a few years and a few miles of each other, in Castleford and Wakefield respectively, Henry Moore and Barbara Hepworth were among the most important 20th-century artists, of Britain as well as Yorkshire.

Moore achieved great wealth and renown across the world from humble beginnings as the son of a mine worker. His father was determined that he should have every opportunity to further himself, and Moore began to carve and sculpt while at Castleford secondary school. After fighting in the First World War he joined Leeds School of Art and won scholarships first in London and then travelling across Italy. Having soaked up influences from great artists of numerous nationalities and techniques, he developed a very individual, abstract style that wasn't always appreciated by early critics. 'The cult of ugliness triumphs at the hands of Mr Moore,' wrote one.

But as he started to sell his work to galleries at home and abroad and to pick up commissions for work to display in public places, Moore's reputation grew – and his appointment as an official war artist in the Second World War brought his work to a wider audience. Though he lived and worked in London and Hertfordshire, he retained his Yorkshire links via exhibitions while winning countless awards and high profile commissions around the world. By the time he died in 1986 he was among the most internationally acclaimed of all British artists, his work featured in dozens of exhibitions a year overseas. In all, he produced close to 1,000 sculptures, and in terms of work on open public display he is one of the most widely known artists of all time.

Moore met Barbara Hepworth at the Leeds School of Art. Born five years after Moore, she, like him, won a scholarship to London, and the pair mixed in the same artistic circles in the capital. Their artistic careers moved in parallel, both in terms of their critical acclaim and success and in their developing styles, which began as quite classical and naturalistic but soon became more adventurous and abstract. She pioneered new approaches to carving and sculpture, and also experimented in collage and photography. Like Moore, she became internationally renowned in the 1950s, and her work is found in public spaces all over the world, including outside the United Nations building in New York. She lived for most of her life in Cornwall, where she died in a fire in 1975.

Sculptures, paintings and drawings by Moore and Hepworth can be found at the excellent Wakefield Art Gallery, and the nearby Yorkshire Sculpture Park also has work from both. Moore's legacy continues through the Henry Moore Foundation, which he set up to promote sculpture and other arts, and the Henry Moore Institute in Leeds. And much of Hepworth's work will be on display at The Hepworth, a major gallery to open in her home town of Wakefield in 2009.

BIRDWATCHING IN YORKSHIRE

Yorkshire's most common birds are the house sparrow and the starling, according to the RSPB's Birdwatch survey. The top five birds for Yorkshire's four regions, plus the average number of times they were spotted in a garden by participants in the Birdwatch survey on one day in 2008, are:

North Yorkshire

1 House sparrow	2.5
2 Starling	1.8
3 Blackbird	1.6
4 Blue tit	1.4
5 Goldfinch	1.4

South Yorkshire

1 House sparrow	2.4
2 Starling	2.2
3 Blackbird	1.4
4 Goldfinch	1.3
5 Blue tit	1.0

East Yorkshire		West Yorkshire	
1 House sparrow	2.6	1 House sparrow	2.3
2 Starling	2.2	2 Starling	2.1
3 Blackbird	1.5	3 Blackbird	1.5
4 Goldfinch	1.3	4 Blue tit	1.4
5 Collared dove	0.9	5 Goldfinch	1.3

YORKSHIRE'S RACECOURSES

Yorkshire has nine racecourses offering flat and jump horse racing around the year. The courses are at:

Beverley

Catterick

Doncaster

Pontefract

Redcar

Ripon

Thirsk

Wetherby

York

A joint website, www.goracing.co.uk, has more information about racing across Yorkshire.

TEN ABBEYS AND PRIORIES

Until Henry VIII's dissolution of the monasteries in the late 1530s Yorkshire was home to dozens of magnificent and influential abbeys and priories. The plundering and neglect of the buildings reduced them to ruins, but today they provide atmospheric evidence of religious life in the county over the centuries. Here are ten of the most interesting remains in Yorkshire, many of them in the care of English Heritage and all accessible to the public.

Bolton Priory, near Ilkley. The 12th-century Augustinian abbey in Wharfedale is part of the popular Bolton Abbey estate, immortalised by

William Wordsworth and J.M.W. Turner. The nave survived the dissolution and continues as the parish church.

Byland Abbey, near Coxwold. A few miles from the more famous Rievaulx Abbey, this was once one of the biggest Cistercian abbeys in Yorkshire, with several hundred monks. The ruins show glimpses of its Gothic elements that inspired other church buildings in the north.

Easby Abbey, Richmond. The Premonstratensian abbey was founded in 1152, by the River Swale and close to Richmond Castle. The refectory and other buildings are well preserved, and the church continues to serve as a parish church.

Fountains Abbey, near Ripon. The Cistercian monastery was founded in 1132 by monks exiled from St Mary's in York. This is one of the best preserved such sites in the country and is part of an estate that has been designated a World Heritage Site.

Kirkham Priory, near Malton. Augustinian ruins by the River Derwent on the edge of the Yorkshire Wolds. The priory and surrounding terrain were used to prepare soldiers and equipment for the D-Day landings in the Second World War and visited in secret by Winston Churchill.

Kirkstall Abbey, Leeds. Founded in 1152 by Cistercian monks from Fountains Abbey, the church, tower, transept and cloisters are very well preserved. Looked after by Leeds city council.

Rievaulx Abbey, near Helmsley. The north's first Cistercian abbey, founded in 1132, and for a long time one of its richest and most important. The substantial remains, by the River Rye in the middle of the North York Moors National Park, are very popular with tourists.

Selby Abbey. Benedictine abbey founded in 1068, the first monastery to be opened in the north after the Norman Conquest. Unusually, it survived the dissolution to continue service as a parish church.

St Mary's Abbey, York. Founded in 1055, rebuilt in the late 13th century, and at one time the biggest Benedictine abbey in northern England. Chunks of the walls remain in the Museum Gardens in the centre of York, and it has served as an atmospheric venue for performances of the York Mystery Plays.

Whitby Abbey. The first monastery here was founded in 657 by a Saxon king and destroyed by the Vikings; the second was built by the Normans and abandoned in the dissolution. The ruins that remain are some of the most atmospheric in England, perched on cliffs above the town and sea.

YORKSHIRE SIMILES

Yorkshire natives are not short of phrases for comparison. Not all of them are unique or native to the area, but here are ten of the more imaginative and popular similes.

As 'appy as a pig in muck

As black as the fire back

As daft as a brush

As dead as a coffin nail

As drunk as a newt

As dry as a lime burner's clog

As gormless as a sucking duck

As quick as an eel

As right as rain

As sick as a Cleethorpes donkey

YORKSHIRE FOOD – FAT RASCALS

They might not have the most politically correct of names, but fat rascals remain one of Yorkshire's most popular teatime treats.

Somewhere between a scone and a rock cake, fat rascals probably got their name not from the children who scoffed them but from their traditional appearance, decorated into a face using cherries and almonds. What sets them apart from plain scones are the currants and fruit zest that are packed into them. They're not exactly healthy, being traditionally made with lard, but they're great with a cup of tea.

There are numerous different fat rascal recipes, including a popular one baked and sold at Bettys tea rooms in York, Harrogate and elsewhere in Yorkshire. This is a fairly simple version.

A recipe for fat rascals
250 g plain flour
100 g butter or lard
75 g caster sugar
75 g currants

finely grated zest of one orange
milk
glacé cherries
sliced almonds

Sift the flour into a bowl. Rub in the butter or lard until the mixture resembles coarse breadcrumbs. Mix in the sugar, currants and grated zest, and add enough milk to get a firm dough. Roll it out on a floured surface to a thickness of about 1 inch (2.5 cm). Cut into rounds as big as you like, and decorate each into a face with the glacé cherries and almonds. Sprinkle the tops with a little more sugar. Place on a baking tray lined with greaseproof paper and bake in a preheated oven, 220°C (425°F), Gas Mark 7, for 15–20 minutes, until golden brown. They are best served fresh, either warm or cooled, split and buttered – with a cup of tea, of course.

ACKNOWLEDGEMENTS

I am hugely grateful to all those who provided ideas and advice as I compiled this book. I am grateful in particular to the staff, publications and websites of the following: the Battlefields Trust, Deliciously Yorkshire, the Department for Environment, Food and Rural Affairs, the Diocese of York, the Dry Stone Walling Association, English Heritage, the English Place-name Society, the Environment Agency, the National Trust, Natural England, the Office for National Statistics, Ordnance Survey, the Ramblers Association, the Royal Society for the Protection of Birds, the Sheep Trust, the Swaledale, Upper Wharfedale and Scarborough & Ryedale fell and cave rescue teams and the Cave Rescue Organisation, Yorkshire Cricket Club, the Yorkshire Dales, North York Moors and Peak District National Park Authorities, the Yorkshire Post, the Yorkshire Ridings Society, the Yorkshire Society, the York Tourism Partnership, the Yorkshire Tourist Board and the staff of Yorkshire's wonderful libraries.

As ever I owe most to my wife, Ceri, for support, patience and love; and to our baby daughter, Beth, for helping in all sorts of ways.

BIBLIOGRAPHY

I am indebted to all those who have researched and written about every conceivable aspect of Yorkshire over the years and who have provided such a vast library of excellent books about the county. This is a selection of some that were most useful to me, and all are warmly recommended for further reading on subjects covered in this book.

Richard Askwith, *Feet in the Clouds: A Tale of Fell-Running and Obsession* (Aurum Press)

Robert Beaumont, *The Railway King: A Biography of George Hudson, Railway Pioneer and Fraudster* (Headline)

David Bellamy, *Dry Stone Walling Techniques and Traditions* (Dry Stone Walling Association)

Derry Brabbs, *James Herriot's Yorkshire* (Michael Joseph)

James Cook, *The Explorations of Captain James Cook in the Pacific* (Dover Publications)

Joe Cooper, *The Case of the Cottingley Fairies* (Pocket Books)

Ann Dinsdale, *The Brontës at Haworth* (Frances Lincoln)

Elaine Feinstein, *Ted Hughes: The Life of a Poet* (Norton)

Mark Fisher, *Britain's Best Museums and Galleries* (Penguin)

Arthur Charles Fox-Davies, *A Complete Guide to Heraldry* (Skyhorse)

Midge Gillies, *Amy Johnson: Queen of the Air* (Phoenix)

Howard Green, *Guide to the Battlefields of Britain and Ireland* (Constable)

William Hague, *William Wilberforce* (HarperPress)

Wilfrid Halliday and Arthur Stanley Umpleby (eds.), *White Rose Garland: An Anthology of Yorkshire Dialect Verse* (Yorkshire Dialect Society)

Ian Hamilton (ed.), *Yorkshire in Verse* (Secker & Warburg)

David Hey, *A History of Yorkshire: County of the Broad Acres* (Carnegie Publishing)

Jeremy Hobson, *Curious Country Customs* (David & Charles)

Bernard Ingham, *Yorkshire Greats: The County's Fifty Finest* (Dalesman)

Simon Jenkins, *England's Thousand Best Houses* (Penguin)

Arnold Kellett, *The Yorkshire Dictionary* (Smith Settle)

Elizabeth Knowles (ed.), *The Oxford Dictionary of Quotations* (Oxford University Press)

Keith Lowe, *The Wonderful Life of William Bradley, the Yorkshire Giant of Market Weighton, East Yorkshire* (Market Weighton Chamber of Trade)

Mary Hanson Moore, *A Yorkshire Cookbook* (David & Charles)

M.C.F. Morris, *Yorkshire Folk-Talk with Characteristics of Those Who Speak It in the North and East Ridings* (A. Brown; o.p.)

John and Anne Nuttall, *Highest Mountains: The Mountains of England and Wales Volume 2: England* (Cicerone Press)

Richard Platt, *Smuggling in the British Isles: A History* (Tempus)

Steve Roud, *The English Year* (Penguin)

Duncan and Trevor Smith, *North and East Yorkshire Curiosities* (Dovecote Press)

Dava Sobel, *Longitude* (HarperPerennial)

Fred Trueman, *As It Was* (Pan)

Isabel Rivers and David Wykes (eds.), *Joseph Priestley: Scientist, Philosopher and Theologian* (Oxford University Press)

Peter Yapp (ed.), *The Travellers' Dictionary of Quotation* (Routledge and Kegan Paul)

The Chambers Book of Facts (Chambers)

The CIA 2008 World Factbook (CIA)

Guinness World Records 2008 (Guinness)

The 2001 Outbreak of Foot and Mouth Disease (National Audit Office)

Foot and Mouth Disease 2001: Inquiry Report (The Stationery Office)

Heartbeat Country (Discovery Guides)

Notes on Building a Cairn: A Leaflet for the Working Waller or Dyker (Dry Stone Walling Association)

INDEX